ANNA MATILDA
'The Urban Nanna'

Everyday Permaculture

Sustainable Living for Every Space

Hardie Grant

EXPLORE

For my dearest Mamma and P'Dads.

Thank you for giving me the best start
possible and for your unfailing support
on my journey to where I am today.
I'm more grateful than I can express.

xo Anna

Contents

INTRODUCTION   4

Chapter 1 Community   20

Chapter 2 Energy   40

Chapter 3 Food   68

Chapter 4 Foraging   132

Chapter 5 Waste   204

Chapter 6 Moving   234

TO NEW BEGINNINGS   250
FURTHER RESOURCES   252
ACKNOWLEDGEMENTS   253
INDEX   254

Introduction

Welcome to *Everyday Permaculture*, a book of important ideas and eco goals transformed into small, adaptable actions.

If you're interested in living a more eco-conscious life, but you don't know where to start or you feel overwhelmed by conflicting advice, this book is written for you. As well as offering loads of tips on how to incorporate permaculture thinking into your everyday life, it covers lots of Big Picture thinking. I hope you'll continue to use this book as a guide for many years as you travel on your journey towards a more sustainable future.

ACKNOWLEDGEMENT OF COUNTRY

I acknowledge the traditional owners of the land I live on – the Wurundjeri Woi Wurrung people of the Kulin nation – and of all the land on which I work. These lands have never been ceded.

I pay my respects to Indigenous Australian Elders past and present, and I will endeavour to preserve, uphold and build from the wealth of traditional knowledge, skills and connection with the land held within the stories and works of Indigenous cultures around the world.

> **Formidable fun**
> Look out for the QR codes in each chapter: they link to funky songs by the band Formidable Vegetable that further explain ideas explored in this book.

THE DAUNTING BIT

With our current knowledge of the urgency of the need for humanity to scale back consumption, rethink approaches to waste, and turbo-boost efforts to regenerate diverse natural ecosystems, it's no surprise that sustainability is top of the agenda for businesses around the globe.

It's been estimated that if every person on the planet were to live like the average Australian, we would need 4.5 Earths to provide the resources required. If we all lived like the average American, 5.1 Earths. Estimates show that collectively, humans are using up Earth's resources 70% more quickly than it can regenerate them, and that figure continues to rise.

The climate crisis is happening, and humans are the only ones who can address it. We ignore that fact at our peril: rising global temperatures affect climate patterns, resulting in an increased occurrence of natural disasters such as droughts, hurricanes and floods. We're already seeing how strings of these catastrophes affect global food supply chains, manufacturing, medicine, infrastructure and biodiversity.

It feels as though we're in chapter 3 of a post-apocalyptic dystopian novel where the narrator explains what caused the downfall of civilisation years before the story is set. But the important difference here is that our future hasn't been written yet. We've still got time to change the narrative.

FEELING YOUR FEELINGS

It's all pretty heavy stuff, and it can lead to a state of overwhelm if you're not careful. 'Eco-guilt' refers to guilt you feel for not doing enough to improve the state of the climate crisis, even if you really want to. There are different types of eco-guilt, and they all feel pretty yuck, but I reckon there's a way they can be turned into a power for good.

Through processes of natural selection, humans have evolved to experience shame and guilt

because they highlight situations where we're not taking actions to protect those around us. This links directly to our in-built imperative to survive, thrive and reproduce: 'If I don't protect others, they might not protect me. Uh-oh! What can I do differently to change that?'

If we acknowledge eco-guilt when it arises (for example, when we buy food with non-recyclable packaging), we can take note of how unpleasant it feels. The next time we do the same thing, we might feel even more guilty. I say good! Hold onto that feeling: let it get stronger every time you do the thing that makes you feel guilty. Eventually, your biological hard-wiring will kick in, and you'll change your behaviour to avoid feeling that guilt ever again.

Having said all of that, it's not good to live in a permanent state of guilt. So while it's important to have an understanding of the bigger picture, we need to have a toolkit of small, slow solutions we can use on a daily basis to help us make incremental positive change without getting bogged down by the heavy thinking.

Rental permaculture
Many books on sustainable living assume that you own the place where you live. But the global reality is that renting where you live is increasingly prevalent. *Everyday Permaculture* has been written to suit renters of all kinds just as well as home owners. Because it doesn't matter whether you own a homestead or rent a room in a sharehouse: there are plenty of simple options for making eco-conscious choices on a day-to-day basis.

'Earth People Fair'

The privilege of living sustainably

Something that's really important to acknowledge when discussing any kind of behavioural change is the diverse range of factors that may affect someone's ability to make said changes. There's a huge amount of privilege embedded in discussions about 'sustainable living', and it's something I don't think is reflected on often enough. Class is typically the biggest element in someone's ability to affect change, as it encompasses so many factors, but there are many other elements to consider.

Here are some factors that might affect someone's ability to implement change in the way they live. I've include just a few possible implications under each, to prompt some deeper thought.

+ **Health and fitness** Access (financial, geographical) to nutritious food; financial capacity to afford good healthcare; food and nutrition literacy; time to cook; injury; access to fitness-building activities; substance addiction (frequently a result of acute life-strain)

+ **Chronic illness** Fatigue; dependency on ultra-packaged medical treatments; need to live near certain facilities; reduced physical strength; brain fog

+ **Ability** Physical disability requiring infrastructure adaptations (ramps, braille signs, captioned announcements etc.); reliance on mobility aids; intellectual disability interfering with critical literacy; memory or impulse control issues; neurodivergence causing overwhelm in certain social settings

+ **Financial stability** Housing (location, safety, security, proximity to work, healthcare and food options); stress levels and associated health issues; time for non-essential activities; capacity to opt for 'more eco-conscious' options; access to education

+ **Older age** Ingrained or unformed thinking on current social norms; lack of technology skills required to safely navigate learning opportunities; lack of 'voice' in society

+ **Gender, race, religion, marginalised status** Access to unbiased information; access to education, healthcare, job opportunities, justice; language barriers; stigmatisation; exclusion or ostracision.

This list is by no means exhaustive, but I hope it will encourage some deep thought about invisible factors that may be affecting others around us. We never really know what's going on in someone else's world. I try to remind myself of that when I see someone doing a thing differently from the way I would do it. Being curious about the actions of others has made me a more tolerant person, and in a world filled with so much busy-ness and hustle and frazzled emotions, there's more need than ever for tolerance.

IS 'SUSTAINABILITY' THE ANSWER?

Many of us grew up learning about 'sustainability' but would be hard-pushed to explain it clearly. You might think, 'It's about recycling. And the environment, and … stuff'.

The term 'sustainability' as we know it today was first used in a text called *A Blueprint for Survival*, published in 1972. Other landmark events for the environmental movement around the same time included the first official Earth Day in 1970 and the formation of Greenpeace in 1971, both of which were the result of the public response to the publication of *Silent Spring* by Rachel Carson in 1962. It has a storied history.

There have been many attempts to define environmental sustainability. My favourite comes from McGill University in Canada: 'Sustainability means meeting our own needs without compromising the ability of future generations to meet their own needs.' Put simply: don't be greedy, and leave some for the next generation.

But is it possible to be truly, wholly sustainable? Fellow permaculture educator Meg McGowan says, 'Our life is so far from sustainable it's not funny. I don't think it's *possible* to live sustainably [in our society]. I aim to [simultaneously] have the least detrimental impact and the greatest positive impact upon the planet', which should arguably be a foundational aim of all humanity.

'Sustainability' and 'sustainable' have been used in business, education, media, marketing and politics since the late 20th century, but their meanings and efficacy have become diluted over time. They're now commonly used in marketing greenwashing, and we're often sold the vague idea that we will 'be sustainable' if we 'just buy this product' or 'vote for that party'. I reckon it's time to tweak our wording and shift our thinking a bit.

What if, rather than trying to 'be sustainable' (which is practically impossible in the modern world), we acknowledged that we're constantly moving 'towards living sustainably'? Why not consistently do the things that are *attainably* sustainable to us, here within this flawed society, and do as much good and as little harm as we can along the way? Carrying out small, attainable and achievable actions puts us in a position of control over the direction we're headed in. It allows room for growth, but also space for mistakes.

I bloody love a mistake, as I maintain it's the best way to really learn something new. By experiencing first-hand what doesn't work, we solidly build our knowledge of what does. If we observe our mistakes, and accept feedback about them, we can then use that feedback to adapt our future behaviour, and increase our potential for overall success. The more we do this, the closer we get to feeling really confident about a new skill. Feeling confident in a range of skills and knowledge allows us to creatively 'use and respond to change', which just so happens to be the 12th principle of permaculture.

Connect the dots
Catie Payne, tiny-house renter on a large-scale homestead, @catieofthesouthernwilds, Australia

'Sustainability means thinking about your place in the ecosystem, what you consume, what you compost, what you contribute – just like any other local creature. Beyond the "shoulds" of sustainability, living in this considered and connective way just feels right.'

What is permaculture?

You may have heard of permaculture, and perhaps you've understood it to be something about gardening and not wearing shoes. But you don't need a composting toilet or a goat to live a permaculture lifestyle: it can be found in city-based manufacturing companies, mainstream schools and regular suburban rental homes. It is, by its very nature, adaptable.

Permaculture is a systems-based framework that has helped people live more ethical, eco-conscious lives for over 40 years. Co-originated by David Holmgren and Bill Mollison in Australia in the late 1970s, it offers a structure by which we can live more in harmony with each other and the planet. At the same time, it guides us as we seek insights and a sense of purpose in our lives. Its central design principles and inbuilt drive to value diversity mean it is highly adaptable, which has led to its adoption and evolution around the globe. These days, permaculture is most often described as a movement.

Many of the foundational ideas of permaculture are deeply rooted and steeped in traditional cultural teachings from all around the world and throughout history. As time goes on, the movement continues to reflect on and learn from Indigenous knowledge and practices wherever it lands. That's why permaculture in Australia looks different from permaculture in the USA or Indonesia: it adapts, evolves and grows organically, shaping communities wherever it's found. In Australia, for example, permaculturalists look to Indigenous knowledge of endemic edible plants and bushfire-risk management with increasing appreciation, and this knowledge is slowly entering standard agricultural and firefighting practice as a result.

I like to think of permaculture as a school uniform: everyone's starts out the same, but the more ours softens and shapes to our body, the more comfortable we feel wearing it. It's designed to let us do the work we need to do, but we can mix and match – or even upgrade – elements of it to help us to achieve different goals at different times. It becomes both a tool *and* an identity that shapes and supports us as we learn and grow.

Before you worry I'll demand that you eat homemade granola and wear only hemp-based clothing (although both *are* pretty great), just know that the reason I bang on about permaculture is because it actually makes it easier to make better ecological choices on a day-to-day basis. You can find a way to make it work for you – patchouli optional.

PERMACULTURE ETHICS AND PRINCIPLES

Permaculture is built on three foundational ethics: Earth care, people care, and fair share. These call on us to look after the planet and all the humans on it, and to aim for balance among all living elements on Earth, as the basis of any action we take.

The ethics framework then branches into 12 guiding principles, shown on page 11. These principles appear broad and possibly a bit vague at first glance, but once you begin seeing them applied to real live actions, it's easy to see how they can help you live a more eco-conscious life, no matter where you call home. I tag almost everything I share on social media with the relevant permaculture principles.

This book isn't a coursebook on permaculture, though, so if you're wanting to learn more about the movement, head to the Further resources section on page 252. But keep the principles and ethics in mind as you read this book: they form the foundation of everything I do and can be seen in action on most pages.

'Limits'

Permaculture principles

1 Observe and interact

2 Catch and store energy

3 Obtain a yield

4 Apply self-regulation and accept feedback

5 Use and value renewable resources and services

6 Produce no waste

7 Design from patterns to details

8 Integrate rather than segregate

9 Use small and slow solutions

10 Use and value diversity

11 Use edges and value the marginal

12 Creatively use and respond to change

LIVING SYSTEMS

This book talks about actions and thinking that can be applied anywhere – caravans, rentals, inner-city apartments, suburban bungalows, rural acreage. That's why I prefer not to use the term 'house' to describe the place where you live. Instead, I often use the term 'living system'. Home ownership is declining, and the increase in both shared situations (e.g. sharehouses and cohousing arrangements) and unconventional living arrangements (e.g. long-term hotel use, caravan park rental or long-term house-sitting) has created a need for a rethink of the term 'home'.

Regardless of the physical structure, the system within which you live usually includes a place to sleep, a place to eat and a place to keep yourself (and your clothes) clean. This might be a house with many rooms and a garden to grow food, but it could just as easily be a houseboat or a room and the use of communal areas in a sharehouse. By using the term 'living system', I hope to encourage you to consider how the actions and ideas in this book may work for you, based on your particular situation.

STACKING FUNCTIONS

In permaculture, 'stacking functions' is a term used to describe a scenario where elements (items or actions) of your living system perform many functions at once. For example, keeping chickens helps reduce food waste, generates food and fertiliser, and helps manage pests and aerate garden soil.

An action that serves multiple functions might be something like having a magnesium bath in the daytime to ease body aches rather than using packaged anti-inflammatory medications: it requires less energy for lighting and water heating than a night-time bath, it uses less water than a shower, my purchase of magnesium flakes supports my local bulk-foods store, the steam and humidity make the pot plants in my bathroom happy, and the cooled water hydrates my garden. Plus it helps reduce stress, meaning I'm more capable of spending my personal energy on things that matter to me.

Essentially, I think about things I want to bring into my living system, and the actions I do, and I try to make each one count in as many ways as possible: I strive to have very few 'single use' things in my life.

It takes a village

In times gone by, a lot of life learning happened in and around the home. Elders taught youngsters to grow and tend gardens, to make and mend garments – and to do the same with relationships, understandings and Community. This method of learning is largely missing in Western society, but it gives me hope to see recent increases in the number of people wanting to reconnect with 'old-fashioned' skills. Foraging, preserving, growing food, bushcrafting, and making and mending clothes are all hot topics in the post-pandemic world.

Learning in person from a trusted elder allows you to assess how their teaching aligns with your values, but that's increasingly difficult with online learning. The rise in AI-generated websites, videos and even books makes critical literacy more important than ever. You can find just about anything online these days, but unfortunately, the sheer volume of information can actually make it harder to learn new-to-you skills effectively. Without someone to inform and guide your online learning, it's difficult to know who to trust.

That's why I think Community is so important. Essentially, I see diverse, connected Community as a vital tool for increased societal resilience. (I look at this in depth in Chapter 1: Community.) If we spend time with people whose values are similar to ours, we feel comfortable making mistakes in front of them. If this were the norm, imagine the learning that could be going on!

My hope for *Everyday Permaculture* is that you will use it to help build your own toolkit of small, eco-conscious actions to use in everyday life. Even more importantly, I hope that it opens your mind to the potential for positive change when we participate in an informed, caring and connected Community.

Introducing me, 'Nanna' Anna

Hopefully, you've asked yourself what gives me the authority to teach you anything. Questioning your sources is, after all, a major part of critical literacy and good learning!

I come from a family fascinated with science, nature and art. My parents taught me that there are no unfixable problems, just ones that we haven't found the solutions to yet. I learned to observe nature through the lenses of both science and art, and from each, I learned that no matter how wild or chaotic something may seem, there's always a system or reason for it.

I learned about foraging from my mum very early on, and dreamt of being a 'forest woman', living off the land and finding everything I needed in the nature around me. As an artist, she also taught me the value of finding beauty and patterns everywhere. My dad taught me that all observations can become data. I watched him finding common ground with whoever he met, which taught me to be generous with my time and attention, as this fosters enriching connections.

I studied botany and horticulture at a tertiary level, which gave me knowledge about plant morphology and behaviours; studying teaching and fine arts allowed me to further my learning in connective thinking and behavioural psychology – both of which are invaluable tools for a permaculture educator. I've been a teacher and leader at a school accredited for its sustainability practices, where I watched students come to life when given the chance to practise hands-on learning and problem-solving

in the permaculture garden. I've also completed several permaculture courses, which is where everything I'd learned kind of slotted together and made sense.

When I left schools, I began developing my skills in growing and preserving food, traditional handicrafts and foraging, which eventually led to the creation of my small business, The Urban Nanna. Through my website, social media, TV, radio and published works, I now teach adults these skills as a way of increasing public engagement in Earth-first, eco-conscious actions.

Coming to a late realisation that I'm autistic went hand-in-hand with developing myself as a permaculture educator. Having spent many years out of step with neurotypical education and social settings, I found that I've got a whole library of lived experience that enables me to help others learn effectively, based on their individual learning style. Watching someone have an 'Aha!' moment is one of my greatest joys, and I love creating rich learning experiences for people of all ages and stages.

As for the 'Nanna' bit of the name, I don't have children of my own, but I've cared for many over the years. Some fun name rhyming came along with that (I'm 'AnnaNanna, my nanny' to some special little dudes), but mostly the grandmotherly title grew from my eagerness to teach children (and adults) in ways similar to how elders used to pass on traditional skills and crafts as part of everyday life.

BEFORE WE START

In Sweden, the word *lagom* (LAH-gom) – which translates roughly to 'just the right amount' – doesn't apply only to how much mashed potato you get on your Ikea lunch plate; it's built into the foundations of Swedish culture and society. It speaks of balance, moderation and finding contentment with 'just enough'. It could be argued that '*lagom* living' is an antidote to consumerism.

Lagom living aligns strongly with permaculture ethics and principles, and it sits firmly within the boundaries of ethical, just and nurturing treatment of all living things. As an autistic science- and art-trained teacher from a Swedish background, I suppose it's inevitable that I'd end up here, using ethics-based systems to help others live contentedly in Community that cares for the health of the planet and each other.

So let's get stuck into it, shall we?

Reflect and moderate
Su Dennett, landowner and homesteader, holmgren.com.au, Australia

'I would love to see us all consider ourselves in a more humble light as to what our needs and expectations are. Do you need your coffee to be perfect, or could you consider running [the coffee grounds through the machine] again? Or could you simply cut your [caffeine] consumption in half? That sort of thinking can help re-establish our individual place within an ecosystem that considers all aspects of the world we live in.'

Chapter 1

Community

The concept of Community has been part of human history for millions of years. Known for more than just its fad-diet way of eating, the paleolithic era saw human ancestors living hunter-gatherer lifestyles, where small groups lived together and divided the labour among all members. They used tools, hunted large game, cooked with fire, and traded items of value with other groups, and it was all done with the express purpose of enabling their group to survive, thrive and reproduce.

Modern definitions of Community describe it as 'groups of people living in the same place or having a particular characteristic in common' and 'the condition of sharing or having certain attitudes and interests in common'. Put most simply, Community is social groups of people who share common interests and values or goals.

Big 'C' Community, little 'c' communities

Historically, communities tended to be geographic, but in the age of digital communication, geography is no longer integral. These days you can't swing your arms without encountering a group of peeps doing something together, whether it's online or in the flesh. Sports clubs, school committees, volunteer groups, online gaming forums, work social groups – they're all made up of people who meet and get along for a specific reason.

To me, there's a distinct difference between communities (with a little 'c') and Community (with a big 'C'). When we talk about communities (little 'c'), they're quite often based on geography, and the word speaks of a group of people gathering together for a specific shared purpose or action. For example, a Landcare community that's focused on cleaning up local beaches. That community is made up of the people who plan and market the clean-up days; the volunteers who turn up to the clean-up days once a month; and potentially the people who make donations to keep the volunteers supplied with bags and gloves.

Community with a big 'C', on the other hand, is broader than that. It's not so much based on what I might do with one set of people; it's more a sense or a feeling I get just from knowing there are different groups out there, invested in doing things to make the world a better place to live.

I feel I am surrounded by Community when I read my local paper, and I see that the primary school near my house is teaching students to compost and grow food; that my council is funding a series of free talks for residents on reducing waste; that the library has invested in creating a 'library of stuff' so people can borrow good-quality tools instead of buying trashy throwaway ones; that my greengrocer stopped plastic-wrapping their produce because so many customers were against it; that a group of people collect the bags and bags of day-old bread from the bakery and take it to one of the many free food-sharing stands in the neighbourhood; that there's a group in my shire lobbying for a local ban on rat bait because the indigenous owls are dying ...

Knowing that there are so many smaller communities swirling and operating around me, each working towards a shared goal of reducing human impact on the planet, and caring for each other, makes me feel a deep sense of groundedness and hope.

My personal sense of Community comes from knowing that all these people exist in my periphery, doing good for each other and the planet. We may be doing very different things with our smaller communities, but we're all committed to finding connection and building strong, resilient groups of humans who feel loved, feel supported, and care deeply about the future.

When viewed this way, Community is more than just the people I hang out with: it's the shape of society around me, reminding me that there are lots of people invested in the same goal, and encouraging me to continue fighting the good fight. It becomes the safety net and the coach at the same time; a lodestar, utopia and nirvana all in one.

Valuing society's margins

Dom Somers, psychologist and critical social worker, Australia

Dom, a single foster parent renting a house in regional Victoria, is a passionate advocate for his Community. He works with vulnerable populations to build connection, wellbeing, belonging and self-determination. He advocates within his local foster-care systems, and he has helped develop and lead grassroots campaigns for independent electoral candidates and First Nations social justice movements. He also contributes to groups advocating for his regional health system, trying to ensure local needs are met into the future.

On barriers to connecting with Community, he says, 'I no longer feel as many barriers to engaging with Community as I used to. Buying into the 'rat race' because of internalised neoliberal motivations left me anxious, fearful and distrusting. The capitalist systems that we're all surviving are also designed to keep us in competition with each other; the opposite of Community. I consciously choose now to live in rural (affordable) spaces, and disconnect from an overly consumerist lifestyle where I can, so that I can afford to work part time. This frees up my time to commit to voluntary actions, which is where the magic of Community happens.'

Why does it matter?

Humans are social beings, which is something many of us came to realise through the early years of the Covid-19 pandemic when lockdowns prevented us from socialising normally. Around the world, consistent feedback from both scientific and anecdotal studies following the lockdowns showed that people of all ages experienced increased levels of insomnia, anxiety, depression and post-traumatic stress disorder. These were particularly felt by people living in complete isolation.

Many other factors, too, affected people during this time, so it wasn't just the isolation of lockdowns that led to poor mental health outcomes, but it definitely contributed. Studies have shown a clear correlation between isolation and sleep disorders, heart disease, a weakened immune system and even premature death. They indicate strong links between health and human connection: which all adds up to indicate that isolation – which could be described as being without Community – is bad for our health.

It follows, then, that Community is good for us. On a primal level, humans need reminders of what it feels like to be part of a bigger picture. Feeling seen, respected and valued makes us believe we matter. This leads to a sense of achievement and success, which is linked to increased endorphins, dopamine and serotonin: the feel-good hormones.

When we connect with others and feel good, it creates a positive feedback loop where we want to replicate what we've felt, so we seek to spread that sense of Community to others, depositing goodwill in their human energy bank, and round and round it goes. Ultimately, building Community has the power to create a better-functioning societal framework, and we're all better for it.

How to build Community

Okay. So that all sounds pretty great, right? But what the heck does it look like, and how can we get some of this feel-good stuff happening?

At its simplest, building Community is as easy as getting to know some of the people in your life a little bit better. Smile or wave at a neighbour; say g'day to someone you've seen a few times at the shops; have a little chat with the postie; stop for a chinwag with someone at your workplace whom you don't spent much time with. Obviously this is going to look different depending on where you live and what shape your life takes, but the general idea is to engage in permaculture principle 1: Observe and interact.

GOOD COMMUNITY IS LIKE A HEALTHY FOREST

Forests are considered to be healthy when they contain a variety of young and old trees of many different species, as well as shrubs, grasses and flowers. When they are rich in plant life, they tend to be rich in other forms of life, from fungi to worms, beetles, birds and mammals.

A biodiverse forest is a sign that nature's cycles, such as the food web, nutrient exchange in the soil, and the water cycle, are working well. When these cycles are in healthy working order, the forest itself is much more resistant to drastic change, disease and destruction.

Community can be viewed through a similar lens: it is strongest and most resistant to disease and destruction when it has healthy cycles of ideas and processes, which come from having genuine diversity in its many members and elements.

Age, race, gender, lived experience, expertise, enthusiasm, ability and interest are all factors that affect Community, and it's important to see patterns and change in their interactions, just as it is with forests. And like forests, Community tends to thrive best in certain places.

Where to find Community

Think of places where people connect and feel better for having a shared interest or shared values. That's where you'll find Community. For example:

+ Online gaming forums

+ Social media groups and followings

+ Professional associations

+ Book clubs

+ Other dog owners at the park

+ RSL or veterans groups

+ Faith or spiritual gatherings

+ Work clubs

+ Regional initiatives

+ Cultural groups and celebrations

+ Sports clubs

+ School parent committees

+ Clean-up crews

+ Local Exchange Trading System (LETS) schemes

+ Intentional communities, sharehouses, cohousing communities and the like.

How to grow your own Community

Aside from joining clubs or classes that charge fees, here are some other ways you can look at growing your own Community forest:

+ Make or engage with street libraries and sharing stands – Food is Free, Grow Free, toys, books, plants

+ Visit local libraries or neighbourhood houses. There's always something happening!

+ Attend local farmers markets and school fêtes to meet locals

+ Join a local walking or nature group

+ See what your council has on offer – most advertise lots of free classes, events, initiatives and gatherings

+ Sign up as a volunteer – retirement villages, churches and animal shelters always need them

+ Start up a project in an area you care about – it might be a poultry club, a pickling group or a letter-writing campaign

+ Join or run a working bee

+ Arrange a street party

+ Share a meal with neighbours, workmates, or people from clubs or groups you belong to.

Trust and diversity: key ingredients of Community

Meg McGowan, permaculture educator, @permacoach, Australia

Meg McGowan facilitates a local community page on social media, and runs a local Produce Share group. She and her partner teach practical skills to locals, like using a chainsaw, building 'cupcake' garden beds (round raised hybrid hügelkultur and no-dig beds), and repurposing old clothing into braided rugs. They also offer assistance to people escaping domestic violence, and host work-for-stay travellers who help manage their permaculture food forest.

'I think the most interesting thing about building Community is that the barriers are a consequence of not having it,' Meg says. 'People worry about loss of privacy or neighbour disputes. They worry that it will be all give and no take. Building Community takes a leap of faith. You need to believe that most people are inherently good and that most people, no matter how different they are to you, would *also* rather live in Community. You need to genuinely value diversity, including the diversity of those that see the world very differently to you. I won't ever be friends with everyone, but I can find a way to engage with them for our collective good.'

Challenges to building Community

In the 1980s a wave of panic about child safety in public spawned the 'stranger, danger' catchcry, and it was drummed into kids that you didn't speak to anyone unless you knew them. This mentality has changed somewhat since then, but for many people born between 1970 and 1990, it's still kicking around as a core memory, much to the detriment of Community. Because how can you build connections and support based on trust if you never trust anyone new?

Another factor hampering the growth of Community in Western society has been the sharp rise of interest in 'prepping' in the past decade, in response to a cocktail of political unrest, increased natural disasters, and the Covid-19 pandemic. Prepping refers to people making preparations for catastrophic events they believe will erode civilisation beyond recognition. Originating in the 1950s during the early years of the Cold War, prepping now sees people install large-scale homestead gardens, build defensible fortresses and stockpile food, medical equipment, weaponry and tradeable commodities with the aim of ensuring their safety 'when the shit hits the fan'.

While there are elements of this kind of 'self-sufficient' preparedness and wariness that can benefit some, I maintain that 'Community sufficiency' offers a far richer and more stable future to work towards. As any gardener will tell you, it's hard work growing all of your own food, and even if it's your full-time job, it's nigh-on impossible to generate *every*thing you need to survive. Stockpiling supplies may sound good in theory, but aside from the money, space and time required to achieve this, it can lead to a scenario of scarcity and panic that has no real foundation. Remember the toilet paper rationing of 2020? I know some people who are still making their way through what they stockpiled. Rather than scrabbling to become self-sufficient, wouldn't it be more beneficial and enjoyable to use our resources to build resilient Community sufficiency instead?

'I can be self-sufficient in ... '   **'I can be community sufficient in ... '**

Catch and store energy

How do we become Community-sufficient, you ask? It's all to do with observing and interacting, using and valuing diversity, and catching and storing energy (those are all permaculture principles – see page 11). And when I say 'energy', I'm not talking about electricity in batteries: I'm referring to human energy and goodwill.

The concept of catching and storing energy in other people is something I learned from the late, great author Terry Pratchett, who wrote a lot about Community, justice and humanity in general. The idea is that when faced with an overabundance of something, like food for example, rather than looking for ways to hoard it and keep it all for your future self, why not put it into other people. The food will be enjoyed at its prime, you won't have to create and then guard a way of storing it, and you will have sown the seed of gratitude in those around you.

While some might see this as frittering away valuable resources, I see it as a kind of banking system for goodwill and kindness. By showing kindness to others and sharing something of real value with them, I can create a Community around me that is predisposed to offer me similar kindness in the future. And once it's started, the goodwill and kindness just keep going round and round.

This approach to building Community helps create a self-sustaining system, where goodwill and resources end up where they are needed most, when they're needed. There's often no formal discussion about it, it isn't tightly governed, and although it isn't a direct trade system, it always seems to work out so people feel like they have enough. We can effectively catch and store *all* kinds of energy in Community, and a great way to get the ball rolling is to start giving.

Stuff: the onerous tenant

Before you worry that I'm going to promote shedding every possession and living in a yurt on a mountainside, know that 'giving' doesn't have to involve tangible things. We all own many more valuable things than we might think.

Time, knowledge, skill, experience, hugs, listening, even a simple smile – these are all resources that can be of value to someone and can be used to grow diverse and resilient Community. In fact, I'd argue that these intangible things are what society actually needs, not more stuff!

I'm a renter, and stuff has always been an issue for me. When it came time for me to move a few houses ago, I realised that one room was full of boxes that were still packed from my previous move. It turned out I'd been paying rent for *two years* to house stuff that I didn't even use.

SET STUFF FREE!

Sure, there are many reasons and privileges tied up in why someone may want or need to keep stuff at different times, and I'd never presume to tell anyone to shed belongings without knowing their situation. But it's worth thinking about the attraction and connection to stuff that we've been raised to have. I've started thinking about stuff in a different way these past few years, and it's brought so many positives into my life.

These days, I've decided I don't want to work long hours so I can earn enough to pay rent on a place where stuff can sit in a box. Instead, I assess whether stuff could be working for me while I don't need it. Essentially, I ask myself, 'Can I send this stuff out into the world where it'll be of use to others, and store some goodwill energy at the same time?' More often than not, the answer is yes. In this way, stuff contributes to the growth of an enriched, connected Community around me and others.

Sharing among neighbours has been around for centuries, and it's interesting to note that you'll often see the most sharing among people who have the least, or when times are toughest.

During pandemic lockdowns of the early 2020s, sharing stands bloomed on suburban streets around the world. Everything from books and toys to homecooked meals, seedlings and even toilet paper appeared in a delightful hodge-podge of shelves and cupboards. People could take what they needed, and shared when they were able.

There are lots of different stands – some free, some swap-based, others set up as honesty stalls where you leave money for goods – but the common denominator is that they are a space where people can access something they need outside of standard consumerist channels.

A box or basket with a hand-written sign just inside your fence may be enough. For ongoing sharing of non-waterproof items (e.g. books or toys), a shelf with protection from the elements would be better.

How to start a Community sharing stand

WHAT YOU'LL NEED

Items you want to share

A way of presenting them

Somewhere safe to share them

Signage of some sort

METHOD

1   Check what sharing stands already exist around you: no point in doubling up.

2   Work out what you want to share, and for how long. This will affect the size and structure of your sharing space.

3   Source a shelf or stand. Online Buy Nothing groups are a great place to hunt, as are tip shops, roadside collection piles and garage sales.

4   Decorate or waterproof the stand, or both. Leftovers of paint can often be picked up free or cheap from people who've been renovating, or you can buy sample pots from hardware stores. Acrylic paint holds up best in the elements.

5   Add brief, clear signage to tell people how to interact with the stand – 'Take a book, leave a book', 'Prices as marked', 'Homegrown produce', 'No packaged food, please'. See page 36 for information on how to make fancy signs easily.

6   Secure your stand to an area inside the boundary line of your property. Make sure it's clear of the footpath, it has no sharp or dangerous elements (e.g. a door that could slam on fingers by accident), and there's no risk of it toppling. This may mean you need to use chains or hardware to secure the stand to something sturdy. A chain threaded through the back of a cupboard and around several fence posts and held tight with a padlock works well.

7   Observe how people interact with the stand for a few weeks. Have a chat with passers-by to explain what it's all about, and answer any questions.

8   Add online elements to your stand if you like. You could create a webpage or social media page that shares information about the stand or collects financial donations to keep it stocked. If you do this, add a QR code or sign with the web address so passers-by know where to look for more info. Do be aware, though, that you'll need to moderate any online spaces, which can become time-consuming.

How to make fancy signs

METHOD

WHAT YOU'LL NEED

A computer or smart device

Paper

A soft graphite pencil

Sign material: a wooden plank, plastic lid, metal tray etc.

Paint: acrylic holds up best in the elements

Brushes (or paint pens).

1   Open an online design app such as Canva on your computer (it's free).

2   Create a new file with the dimensions of your sign.

3   Type what you'd like to include, pick a font and play around with the formatting till you're happy.

4   Download the file as a jpeg. Flip the digital image horizontally so it's 'back to front'.

5   Print the file on paper at actual size (no scaling).

6   On the reverse side of the paper, fill the outline of the printed letters with soft graphite pencil.

7   Lay the paper graphite-side down on the sign and secure it with tape or clips.

8   Trace over the letter outlines firmly. This transfers the graphite image to the sign beneath.

9   Remove the paper. Go over the letters on the sign with paint pens or paint and a brush.

10 Voila!

Don't have a printer? Try using your computer screen as a light box! Follow the instructions above to the end of step 4. Cut the paper to the size you want, place it on the screen with the reversed image showing at full size, trace gently around the letters in soft pencil, then lay *that* side down on your sign and scribble over the top of the page. This transfers the traced outline onto the sign.

Share and share alike

By sharing my stuff around, I can afford a slightly nicer rental, because I don't need to house as much stuff. It also doesn't take me as long to pack, or cost as much to move as it did before. Overall, I've saved money and gained time to do what's important to me, *and* I've nourished a Community that may one day give me support in a time of need.

The concept of a 'gifting economy', which is prominent in permaculture communities, sees people trading and bartering with all sorts of things. You might see a loaf of bread and a dozen eggs being traded for half an hour cleaning out the gutters; or someone might swap some indoor plants they propagated for a few driving lessons. Carpooling arrangements for school pick-up and drop-off, help building a garden deck for a slab of beer, taking it in turns to host catch-up dinners: it's entirely likely that you're already trading in the gifting economy without even realising it.

There are formal systems based on this model, such as LETS (Local Exchange Trading System), BarterCard and BizX, but more often than not, once people start recognising and redistributing wealth this way, generosity begets generosity and it just keeps going around.

When I think about my 'earning' and 'spending' capacity in terms of my expertise and stuff, I honestly feel not only rich but enriched. People will happily trade things I need for the stuff I want to share – and for my skills and knowledge too. And the best thing is that the people I'm exchanging with are enriched by this system too.

'Our Street'

Building Community: the takeaways

1   Look around your life and really *see* what's happening out there. Find a local group to join (or start one). Start connecting with humans around you.

2   Think of yourself as someone who has 'things worth sharing'. This could be stuff, skills, time etc.

3   Start sharing! Trade if you like, but remember that if you trust in the process and give freely with no expectations, the give-and-take all works out in the end.

4   Growing healthy Community takes time. Start to build it *before* you have need of it. And enjoy the 'forest' as it grows.

Chapter 2

Energy

'Energy is everything and everything is energy' is a brilliant reminder that everything in our lives is connected in ways we can't immediately see. It can be used to shed light on several permaculture principles, including 'Obtain a yield' and 'Use and value renewable resources and services'. It also touches on the importance of stacking functions (see page 12) and conserving energy by valuing what's embodied in objects and resources around us. Essentially, it gets us thinking about what energy actually is, how it's generated, what it looks like, and how we can best value it.

What is energy?

Energy can be simply described as 'the ability and strength required to do work'. The law of conservation of energy (a principle of physics) states that it can be neither created nor destroyed, but can only be converted from one form to another. There are many different types of energy, according to science – heat, light, motion, electrical, chemical and gravitational – and these forms of energy can be categorised as with potential (stored) or kinetic (working) energy.

As humans, we've become pretty good at converting different types of energy in ways that other living organisms can't. For example, we take potential chemical energy from wood or coal and convert it to kinetic heat energy for our homes and cooking, and we use the gravitational energy of water in hydroelectric systems to produce electricity. But when we rely on non-renewable energy sources like coal or natural gas, we're running a losing race.

The population of humankind is so vast that there simply aren't enough non-renewable resources to go around. This is why it's so important to start thinking about not only how to reduce our overall use of energy, but also how to make the most of passive and embodied energy in our day-to-day life.

Where does energy come from?

Sources of energy are many and varied, and there are pros and cons to most of them. Non-renewable sources include coal, oil, natural gas and nuclear energy: once these resources are used up, they can't be replaced. Renewable sources include things like wind, solar, geothermal and hydroelectric energy.

Thinking about energy can feel like being back in school, learning stuff that's not really that interesting to you. And it's difficult to find unbiased information, because lots of what's out there comes from energy supply companies, whose main objective is to get your money. Getting a true understanding of how to lower your carbon footprint when it comes to energy consumption can feel too hard.

That's where permaculture thinking can help! 'Design from patterns to details' (principle 7) and 'Use and value renewable resources and services' (principle 5) might sound academic, but boiled down, all they mean is 'Choose a big picture of how you want to live, then work out how to create it' and 'Use stuff that doesn't run out and don't be greedy'. When I'm thinking about energy consumption, I find these principles useful, because they keep bringing me back to basic thinking no matter what the situation.

'Energy'

Let's get personal

Before launching into how to manage energy efficiently, I want to touch on human energy, by which I mean things like physical strength, emotional capacity, knowledge, skills, time, love and care, Community power, and even respect. While these may be difficult to quantify scientifically, it's easy enough to tell when they're in deficit. I think about them the same way I think about other forms of energy: they're valuable resources that can be built up, saved, spent, and – if we're not careful – exhausted.

As a late-diagnosed Autist, and living with anxiety and occasional depression, I've had times where my human energy has bottomed-out, and I've struggled to perform basic daily tasks. At these times, I certainly didn't have the energy to spend making the most energy-conscious choice while shopping for food: sometimes it took all I had just to get to the shop in the first place. Rather than feel guilty, though, I've come to think of that as me doing the best I could with the human energy I had at my disposal.

Being someone who lives alone, rents, and runs an educational business, I've learned I *have* to be aware of my personal energy. If I don't predict and plan for times when external forces might become overwhelming, I run the risk of being left with insufficient energy to do all the things I need to do. Something called Spoon Theory is really handy when thinking about this sort of stuff.

SPOON THEORY

In case you're unfamiliar with Spoon Theory, here's the lowdown on the term coined by Christine Miserandino, an American writer who lives with chronic illness.

Every action in a day – whether it be mental or physical – uses a certain number of personal energy units. Each of these units can be represented by one spoon. People living with chronic illness, disability, significant mental health challenges or neurodiversity have a limited number of spoons they can use each day, whereas people living without challenges like these have an almost unlimited supply.

People with fewer spoons at their disposal often experience overwhelm, but over time, they can develop ways to manage, budget and replenish their spoons. They may ask for help performing physical tasks; request accommodations in workplaces or learning spaces that mean they don't have to filter out as many external stimuli; set up systems in their daily life that make the best use of the spoons they have; create 'escape hatches' for when they're down to their last spoon; or do certain activities that help them replenish their stores after a particularly spoon-hungry event.

This could look like holding a working bee or asking a friend to body-double to help them as they complete a physical task; using mobility aides, tinted glasses or noise-cancelling headphones; scheduling alone-time before and after a social event; or getting takeaway – even if it comes with unsustainable plastic packaging – to ensure they have energy to complete a larger sustainability-focused activity.

Spoon Theory is useful when we're seeking to make sustainable changes to the way we live, because it reminds us that we can't do it all, all the time. Making a choice to transition to a lower-waste, more eco-conscious way of living is great, but if we try to do it all at once with not enough spoons, it'll be almost impossible to maintain.

So when it comes to thinking about the energy in your living system, consider adding your personal brand of human energy to the list. Use it to help you moderate and apply self-regulation to your actions, so that you've got enough 'spoons' to go the distance.

Measuring out your 'spoons'

Tanya van der Weert, a student in Australia, rents a medium-scale rural homestead and has observed that sometimes the best choice isn't the most energy-efficient choice.

'As a full-time student, I've chosen to minimise the paid work I do in order to focus on getting the best out of my studies,' says Tanya. 'If I was more financially secure I'd have many more options in terms of buying land, buying an electric vehicle etc. Health limitations really impact on the amount I can work, but also on my capacity day-to-day to complete chores. I make mindful, long-lasting and ethical spending choices when it comes to resources like furnishings, clothing and food, but sometimes, the absolute best thing you can do for yourself might *not* be the most frugal or most energy-efficient choice. Sometimes you need to take a really long, hot shower. Sometimes you need to get takeaway. Sometimes turning on the heater on a not-super-cold night, because you're overtired and sore and chilled to the bone, is actually what you need. I think it's really, really important to allow ourselves grace by recognising that sometimes we need to do things outside of our aspirations, and that's okay.'

Energy at home

With the rising cost of living and predicted increase in climate fluctuations, it makes sense to look to your home as a place where you can reduce your energy usage and thereby your overall carbon footprint. Reducing the amount of electricity, gas and water you use on a daily basis not only saves money but reduces the need for service providers to supply you with those resources. The less supply needed, the lower the overall impact on the environment.

Your living space is also the best place to really start paying attention to stacking functions (see page 12), identifying 'passive' energy, and making the most of energy in general. When you use energy in your home, you immediately reap the benefits of it. And because you generally then have to pay the bill for the supply of that energy, you tend to be acutely attuned to the cause and effect of your energy consumption. This is the perfect springboard from which to begin looking at how to make the absolute most of energy – passive, embodied or purchased.

Stacking firewood and stacking functions

Catie Payne lives in a tiny house on a large-scale Australian homestead, where the work required to keep her wood stove burning gives her acute insights into her own energy use.

'Having a tiny space brings giant energy benefits,' says Catie. 'One room doesn't take much lighting or heating, and solar-passive design helps immensely. I conserve energy through behavioural changes too, exercising to warm up, wearing lots of snug clothing, batch-cooking meals, being aware of doors, windows and drafts, and being okay with a little discomfort.

'I have a wood stove, and that wood stove cooks my food, heats my home and provides hot water. From going out into the forest and hauling fallen timber onto our truck, to splitting the wood and lighting the stove, I have an acute awareness of how much wood energy (and human energy) it takes to bake a cake or fuel a hot shower. If my fire's on, I'm stacking as many pots on top as possible, eking out that lovely warm water for days upon end. First-hand participation in my energy system has made me a very mindful consumer indeed.'

HOME ENERGY AUDIT

Before you can make any kind of meaningful change – whether it be behavioural or strategic – it's important to know what's already happening, what works well, and what doesn't. When it comes to energy, one of the simplest ways to get this information is with a home energy audit.

Around the world, it's now possible to buy or rent home energy audit kits, which can help you analyse where and when energy is lost or wasted in your home. Check with your local library and local government before you go out and buy one.

Electricity 'smart meters' are increasingly available, and some electricity providers now offer apps where customers can track their usage live, allowing them to identify times when they're using the most electricity. Check with your energy provider.

BE REAL

Once you've worked out where you're using and losing most of your energy, it's time to make clear plans on how you'll change things. Remember, small, incremental changes will always be more achievable and more likely to stick, so don't try to do everything at once.

Think realistically about your day-to-day life. If you're low on personal energy 'spoons', perhaps don't try to implement a change that requires you to do something new every day: chances are you'll do it for a few days, quickly begin to resent it, and eventually let it slide completely, never to be taken up again. Rather, choose an action that you can do once to get long-lasting benefits from, like adding a door-snake or mounting a pelmet above a window to reduce draughts that would normally cause you to turn on (or turn up) the heater or air-con.

MAKING SMALL CHANGES

We all know we can reduce energy wastage by doing things like turning off lights when leaving a room, and installing energy-efficient light globes and appliances, but that doesn't always equate to *doing* them in our home.

To get you started, here's a checklist of small, simple energy-saving actions to consider.

+ Install energy-efficient light globes (LEDs use the least power)

+ Switch off lights and appliances when not in use

+ Identify and manage 'vampire appliances' (see page 51)

+ Block or seal gaps around doors and windows

+ Fit water-saving taps and showerheads

+ Set thermostats (heating, cooling, hot water) appropriately

+ Check seals on appliances such as the fridge.

Once you've ticked off a few of these, you can start changing some of your daily habits to help keep energy usage low, and to maximise every bit you use. There are some basic things that can apply across all areas of a home, such as servicing appliances so they're working optimally, managing your body temperature rather than trying to change the temperature of a large room, and being sure to investigate energy-efficient appliances whenever something needs to be replaced. Ultimately though, using a range of small and slow solutions is an excellent way to increase your home's overall energy efficiency.

'Small & Slow'

Vampire appliances

'Vampire appliances' are things that draw a significant amount of energy even when you're not using them. Typically, these are larger electrical items left on 'standby', such as TVs, gaming consoles and desktop computers. If it's ready to power up at the slightest touch, there's a fair chance it's continuously using energy. Send a metaphorical stake through its heart by switching off each vampire appliance at the wall.

ROOM BY ROOM

To help you with this, here's a room-by-room look at changes and habits you can try implementing. There's plenty in here that I've done as retrofitted, portable solutions in rentals, so don't think you have to suffer in shivering (or sweltering) silence if you don't own where you live. If you're a check-a-box kinda person, head to urbannanna.com where you'll find a free checklist you can download to help you track your progress.

Living spaces

+ Fittings and appliances

Look to insulation to stop the transfer of heat. Checking, installing or improving ceiling, wall and underfloor insulation is great, but you can also achieve a lot with fabric wall-hangings and rugs to reduce heat-loss in winter.

To minimise transfer of heat through windows, investigate double-glazing (available as a removable or permanent option) but also get into some curtain and blind action. Use good-quality blackout curtains, as these insulate really well, or look at honeycomb blinds, which trap heat between their layers. Use blind locks at the base of windows to stop roller blinds flapping about and letting heat in or out. You can find cheap secondhand curtains in op shops or from Buy Nothing groups online. You can even take the curtains you buy with you from house to house if you're renting so a good investment isn't lost.

Create separate spaces within large rooms, so you can focus on managing the temperature in a smaller area. You can use bookcases, screens or room dividers to achieve this. Many rentals have had doors removed, but simply hammering in a few nails on top of the door frame and attaching a thick blanket replaces them quite effectively. Fit door seals and draught-stoppers, and close off areas that aren't used much.

Use fans before turning to air-con, and use the most energy-efficient mode available. If you have ceiling fans, check whether there's a summer and winter switch. In summer mode, fans draw hot air up away from the room; in winter mode, they push rising warmth back down to where it's needed.

Monitor and moderate appliance usage. Avoid using lots of appliances in summer, as they generate heat which may result in you wanting to use air-con. Choose the most efficient lighting for your needs: for example, a small reading lamp with an LED globe uses less energy than multiple overhead lights, and may be all you need. Use powerboards with individual switches and turn off anything not in use. Have your appliances serviced regularly to ensure they work as efficiently as possible.

+ Habits

Learn to adjust your temperatures in the simplest way possible: don't rely only on appliances. For example, add extra clothing layers in winter (or remove layers in summer), then give it 30 minutes before you decide whether you need to turn on (or up) the heating or cooling. In winter, move around more and use blankets to warm your body, and in summer, move less and move more slowly to avoid overheating.

Learn and limit how heat moves in and around your home. Heat always wants to travel towards cold, so wherever there's an 'edge' between indoors and outside – doors, floors, windows, external walls – that's what it will try to do. If it's hot outside, heat is going to try to get into the house, and vice versa. In summer, you can help stop heat from moving into and through a house by closing curtains and internal doors on a hot day. This creates smaller spaces that can be cooled using less energy than a large area.

The only way is up

If you have venetian blinds, angle the slats according to the season: up in summer, down in winter, as heat rises and travels in whichever direction the slats are pointing.

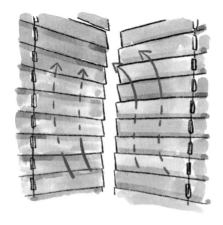

Kitchen

+ Fittings and appliances

Enable appliances to work optimally and efficiently. Defrost freezers regularly and set their temperature to suit the contents. Avoid overfilling fridges and freezers, as they guzzle energy to keep things cold if overstuffed. Check seals on appliances and replace if damaged. Service your appliances regularly.

Minimise the amount of energy you use. Slow cookers, smaller ovens and air-fryers use less energy than traditional larger appliances. Note that if you use an air-fryer to make a recipe written for an oven, you may need to adjust the temperature or cooking times. 'Haybox' or 'hotbox' cooking is a very savvy way to cut down energy use and is super-simple (see page 54). Fill the kettle with only as much water as required so it uses less energy to boil, or fill a thermos with boiled water to use throughout the day for tea and coffee rather than boiling the kettle many times.

Look at adapting your kitchen decor to suit the seasons: use floor mats, blinds and curtains in winter, and external or internal shading in summer.

+ Habits

Make the most of the energy you use for cooking. Line up a series of things to cook in an oven once it's already hot rather than heating it up many times. 'Stack functions' to optimise energy use: for example, steam broccoli in a basket above a pot of boiling potatoes, then use the cooled water on the garden. Leave the oven door ajar after cooking to heat the kitchen in winter, or use it to dehydrate food. Avoid using appliances such as the dishwasher and the oven when they're only half-filled.

Time cooking effectively. Cook just before you'll eat to reduce the need for reheating. Use lids and covers to conserve heat when cooking. In winter, consider cooking over fire that doubles as heating. In summer, avoid cooking with heat during the day, and either batch-cook during cooler times of the day, or prepare meals that don't require heating, such as salads and wraps.

Use it up. Learn to value the embodied energy in food and packaging in the kitchen. Use up every bit of food, employ reusable storage and packaging, and repurpose commercial packaging where you can.

Use and reuse water wisely. Install water-saving taps. Wash fruit and vegetables in a tub or bowl, then use that water on the garden. Wash dishes by scrubbing them with a sudsy brush, popping them in the sink, and then rinsing them all together, rather than filling the whole sink or washing and rinsing each one while the tap is running.

Bedrooms

+ Fittings and appliances

Use natural fibres in bedding and floor coverings. Rugs, blankets, quilts and sheets in wool, down, linen, cotton and flannelette will all help moderate temperatures and reduce the need for powered heating or cooling. In contrast, manufactured fabrics like polyester don't allow your skin to 'breathe', leaving you clammy, and they don't hold heat when you want them to either.

+ Habits

Heat or cool your body rather than the whole room. Take a cool shower before bed in summer, and a hot one in winter. Wear temperature-appropriate bedclothes (thermals and socks in winter, perhaps nothing at all in summer). Use wheat packs or hot water bottles instead of an electric blanket. Add an extra blanket to the bed in winter and sleep under just a sheet in summer. Go to bed a bit earlier, or lie in later during the cooler months: sniggle-snuggling under a doona is a heck of a lot cheaper than putting on the heater!

Think inside the box

The Norwegian method of slow cooking known as 'hotbox' cooking uses a heavily insulated box to cook food using residual heat. It dates from 1867 and is just as useful today as it was back then. The method involves simply combining ingredients in a heavy lidded pot, bringing them to a rolling boil on a stovetop, then placing the pot in a box lined with a thick layer of felt, hay, or any other good insulating material. (During World War I, the method was known as haybox cooking.) The residual heat will continue cooking the food slowly over many hours. For food safety reasons, use a cooking thermometer to ensure the temperature of the food doesn't dip below 60°C/140°F.

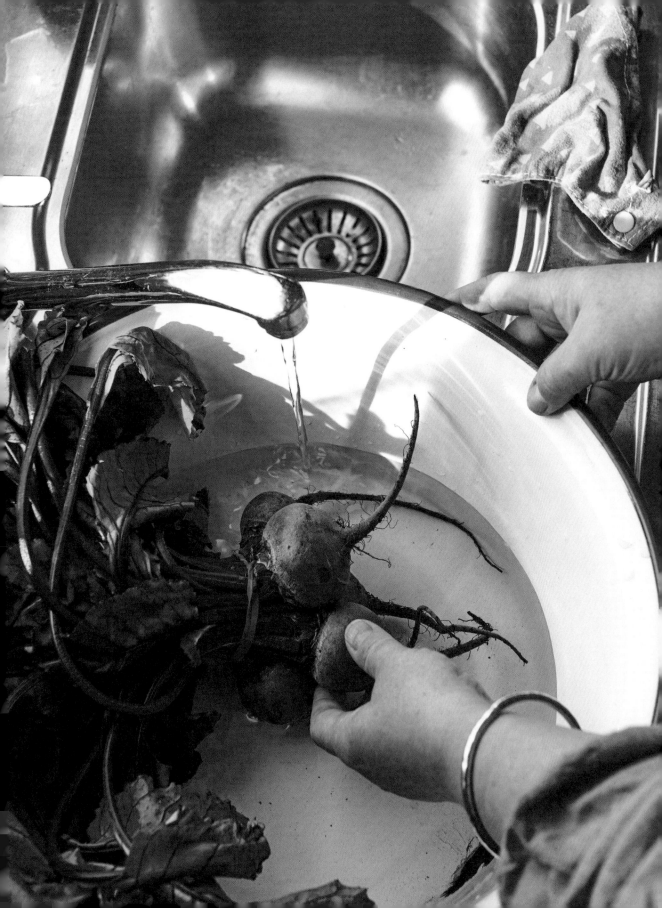

Bathrooms

+ Fittings and appliances

Insulation is key in bathrooms. Double-glazing is absolutely worth it, but if that's out of budget, a cheap, reversible option is to stick bubble-wrap to windows, especially in winter. Using floor mats can reduce the need for electric heating.

Install water-saving showerheads and taps.

+ Habits

Reduce the need for excessive hot-water heating by taking shorter showers, or shower on alternate days. Reduce the temperature on the hot-water heater thermostat by one or two degrees.

Reduce water loss by collecting cold water in a bucket as the shower heats up: this can be used to run a cold wash in the laundry, or water a garden. Avoid overfilling baths, especially when bathing children. Use grey-water-safe soaps so you can use bathwater to water fruit trees and ornamental gardens. Turn shower taps down slightly to reduce the amount of water being used per second.

Laundry

+ Fittings and appliances

If you're buying a washing machine, choose an energy-efficient front-loader with the capacity to wash efficiently with cold water: they use significantly less water and electricity than top-loaders. If you have a garden, consider fitting a flexible pipe to your washing machine outlet and using the water to hydrate ornamental garden beds, lawns or trees. Make sure to use grey-water-safe detergents if you do this.

Air-dry clothes, using racks, clothes horses or washing lines, indoors or out. Avoid electric dryers wherever possible as they churn through energy.

+ Habits

Wash clothes and soft furnishings as directed, which usually means washing them less often than you expect. Cutting down on frequency not only reduces the need for water and electricity, but means clothes last longer too. Learn to treat stains before adding them to the washing machine, and consider handwashing smaller items or loads.

Master your washing machine. Avoid under- or over-filling, learn which settings give optimal results, and use grey-water-safe and septic-safe detergents, which are gentler on your machine, your clothes and the environment.

Seven ways to rethink and reuse stale bread

Bread has been a staple of human diets in one form or another for thousands of years, and there are just as many different recipes out there for making your own. Making bread is actually an incredibly energy-hungry activity, so each slice holds a tremendous amount of embodied energy. Throwing away stale bread, therefore, is wasteful from more than one angle.

As with many food commodities, high demand for bread leads to regular surplus, which results in massive waste. Day-old bread has been sold cheap or donated to charitable organisations in Western countries for centuries, but better still is drawing on a variety of ways to use up stale bread so it's no longer viewed as part of a waste stream that needs managing. Here are seven ways to use bread when it's too old to make into sandwiches.

Breadcrumbs

METHOD

1   Break bread into smallish pieces and spread on oven trays in a single layer.
2   Toast in an oven at 100°C/212°F until thoroughly dried out (10–15 minutes).
3   Cool, then crush into small crumbs by rubbing firmly between your hands or running through a food processor.
4   Store in an air-tight jar in the pantry.

How to revive stale bread

This method of reviving stale bread works best on large pieces with lots of crust. It's not ideal for sliced bread.

METHOD

1   Preheat the oven to 200°C/400°F.
2   Run the bread under a cold tap until it's wet all over but not soaked.
3   Place it on an oven tray and bake until the crust is crisp (about 10 minutes). Alternatively, warm it in a microwave. Wrap the bread in a clean tea towel (dish towel) and microwave it in 10-second bursts until it's soft and springy (20–30 seconds).

Panzanella salad

Kind of like a deconstructed bruschetta, this salad is perfect for a quick summer lunch. It's great made with stale sourdough. The quantities are very loose, and you can adjust the proportions to your taste.

METHOD

1   Chop some juicy, ripe tomatoes, spring onions or red onion and feta into a bowl.

2   Tear some stale bread into chunks and add.

3   Tear some basil or mint leaves, add them to the bowl and mix everything well.

4   Make a basic vinaigrette with olive oil, balsamic vinegar, crushed garlic, salt and pepper. The bread will absorb the dressing, so be sure to allow for this. Pour the vinaigrette over the salad and mix well.

5   Set aside for 5–10 minutes to allow the flavours to meld, then serve.

Bread and butter pudding   Serves 4

This is a great way to use up stale white bread, raisin toast or hot cross buns.

INGREDIENTS

6–8 slices stale bread

1 cup milk

¾ cup pouring cream

2 eggs

⅓ cup sugar

2 tbsp melted butter, cooled, plus extra butter for topping

½ cup sultanas (golden raisins)

1 tsp cinnamon

Icing sugar (confectioner's sugar), for dusting

METHOD

1   Preheat the oven to 180°C/350°F.

2   Tear the bread into chunks.

3   Lightly whisk the milk, cream, eggs, sugar and melted butter in a bowl until combined.

4   Add the bread and sultanas and set aside to soak for 2–3 minutes.

5   Transfer to a baking dish, top with a few knobs of butter and sprinkle with cinnamon.

6   Bake for 25–30 minutes, until golden.

7   Dust with icing sugar and serve with ice cream.

Parmesan crackers

These are best made with bread rolls or breadsticks.
They're brilliant for cheese platters.

METHOD

1   Slice the bread into pieces 1–2 cm/⅜–¾ inch thick.

2   Brush both sides of each slice with olive oil.

3   Lay the slices flat on a baking tray.

4   Grill (broil) on medium heat until golden (about 4–5 minutes).

5   Flip the slices over, sprinkle some parmesan on top of each one and pop them back under the grill.

6   Grill until the parmesan is bubbly and golden (about 3–4 minutes).

7   Transfer to a cooling rack. Once cooled, store in an airtight container for up to a week.

Old-school booze

Makes about 4 cups

Rye kvass is a simple fermented drink made with burnt rye bread, which takes on a stout-like flavour once brewed. It is mildly alcoholic, so enjoy it in moderation.

INGREDIENTS

⅓–½ loaf stale rye bread

5 cm strip of orange zest

5 cm nub of unpeeled ginger, sliced

2 tsp raw honey

2 mint leaves

3–4 juniper berries

METHOD

1   Slice the bread into thick slices.

2   Toast in a toaster, under the grill or over flames until well toasted and blackened in parts.

3   Crumble the toast into pieces and place them in a large jar (it should be half full). I use a jar that holds 1 litre (4 cups). Fill the jar with cold water.

4   Add the orange zest, ginger, honey, mint and juniper berries. Seal and shake.

5   Leave the jar to ferment at room temperature for three to five days. Shake and 'burp' the jar daily (open it to let the carbon dioxide out, then reseal).

6   Strain and bottle the kvass. Pop the bottles in the fridge for a couple of days to build up some bubbles, then enjoy.

Garlic herb croutons

These croutons are my favourite way to use stale sliced bread in the cooler months. Measure the seasonings with your heart – I use around 1 teaspoon of herbs and ½ teaspoon of garlic powder per 4 slices of bread.

METHOD

1   Preheat the oven to 180°C/375°F.

2   Cut the bread slices – as many as you like – into 3 cm/1¼ inch squares.

3   Toss them in a bowl with enough olive oil so that each piece is lightly coated.

4   Add some dried mixed herbs, powdered garlic, salt and pepper and toss until all the pieces have a herby coating.

5   Spread the bread in a single layer on a baking tray. Bake until golden on all sides (10–12 minutes), turning the bread occasionally.

6   Serve with soups or on top of salads.

7   Leftover croutons can be stored in an airtight jar for up to a week, but they're best eaten fresh.

GET AGGRESSIVELY PASSIVE

Using passive energy is something you probably already do, even if you don't realise it. In its simplest form, it involves using natural energy such as sunlight or wind to perform a task with no intervention from powered equipment. Drying your clothes on a clothesline outside makes use of both passive solar and passive wind energy. Spending your winter days in rooms with north-facing windows (south-facing in the northern hemisphere) makes use of passive solar energy to keep you warm.

If you have the ability to build or renovate where you live, investigating passive heating and cooling during the design phase could save you a bundle in bills over the years. Passive solar houses have features such as windows that catch and store thermal energy during winter so it can heat the house, and that stop the sun from reaching them during summer. There are also designs that make use of strategically placed windows, doors and vents to channel airflow and keep the house cool.

If building or renovating isn't on the cards for you, there are still plenty of ways to make use of passive energy with existing structures. With a little bit of know-how, you can use doors and windows to channel air and sunlight and effectively heat and cool your house. Using heat-absorbing materials like concrete, tiles and metal to dry clothes, dehydrate food and even cook food is pretty simple. Following the sun from room to room to keep warm if you work from home is another trick. Keeping track of hot and cold areas in your space throughout the year is a good way to unearth potential energy hotspots. So when an area feels too hot or cold, make a note of it, and start thinking of how you could harness that passive energy for active use.

Drying food with passive energy

Part of learning how to manage energy efficiently in and around our living systems is understanding that everything is connected one way or another. If we're actively 'spending' energy on something that doesn't give us *at least* that much energy in return, it's not an energy-efficient action.

Drying food is a great example of this. Commercial dehydrating machines use electricity, which can become expensive (and contribute to environmental problems) if you're using them often. Fortunately, there are several ways to dehydrate food using passive energy sources. By using these methods, we can 'catch and store (food) energy' (permaculture principle 2) without expending electrical energy.

+ Making a small-scale solar dehydrator

Lay out slices of fruit or vegetables on something flat and place it somewhere warm and sunny during the day. Bring it in at night, and repeat as necessary until the food is dried to your liking.

You can use flat baskets, a baking tray lined with a clean tea towel (dish towel) so the food doesn't burn on the metal, or even a well-cleaned flyscreen.

You want as much heat as possible when dehydrating outdoors. You can utilise the thermal mass captured in concrete, bricks, pavers or even a metal or tiled roof by placing your set-up on top of these materials. Airflow is also important, because you want evaporated moisture to move away from the food. Popping your basket on a table or some bricks can be enough. One excellent place to put baskets is on top of the washing line, which in most properties is positioned in the sunniest spot. Choose a day that's not too windy and lay the basket across several strands of the line.

If you have birds and beasties around, cover the food lightly with light fabric such as cheesecloth, scarves, tea towels or muslin to keep them at bay.

+ Making a larger scale solar dehydrator

You can construct a solar dehydrating unit using repurposed or secondhand materials. This could be as simple as an old greenhouse with a mesh instead of plastic cover and some extra wire shelves; or you could build a timber and glass frame with a reflective panel to accurately channel the sun's heat through the unit. The internet offers loads of designs.

+ The dashboard method of dehydration

The dashboard of a car makes an excellent place to dehydrate things like herbs and flowers. Line the dash with clean paper or tea towels (dish towels), spread out the food, and park the car somewhere sunny for the day.

This is *not* a method to use for drying chillies or garlic: the smack-in-the-face garlic aroma and chilli fumes in the eyes make driving safely difficult for a week afterwards.

+ Solar dehydration indoors

This super-simple method is great for houses or apartments with windows that face north or west (or in the northern hemisphere, south or west). Place a table directly next to the window and lay out trays or baskets of fruit, veg, herbs or flowers so the sun falls on them throughout the hottest part of the day. If it gets chilly and damp by the window overnight, move the food away when the sun sets so it doesn't reabsorb moisture.

A European folk method of drying food indoors was to string it up and festoon the windows with delicious garlands. Chillies, mushrooms, edible flowers, bunches of grapes or elderberries, and small posies of herbs all work well. Thread a large needle with foodsafe cotton string a little bit longer than your window is wide, then use the needle to pierce through the thickest part of each item until you have half-filled the string. Attach the ends of the string to opposite sides of the window and space the food out evenly along it so there is plenty of room for airflow.

This method isn't suitable for food containing lots of moisture, as it can sag and fall off the string as it dries.

+ Dehydrating indoors with secondary heat: stacked functions

Most indoor living spaces have some form of heat source, whether it's an oven, a wood fire, or gas or electric heating. These sources aren't technically 'passive' because they require an active input of energy to produce heat, but if we're already using them to perform another function, then stacking functions and using the ambient heat around them is still a savvy way of maximising energy use. Heaters, fireplaces and ovens are great places to use secondary heat for drying food.

Dehydrating with your heater or fireplace

Use the warm air around heaters or fireplaces to dry bunches of herbs or flowers, or baskets and trays of sliced veg or fruit. Hang the bunches from a clothes horse in front of the heat source, or string them up above it. You can pop leafy greens into a metal colander and position it above the heat source. Place the baskets or trays where they'll have warmth and airflow circulating around them.

Oven dehydration

If your oven gets a workout daily, use the residual heat after cooking to dry food over several days. Lay the prepared food out on trays lined with cooling racks (to allow airflow), and slide them in once the temperature drops to 100°C/212°F. Leave the oven door ajar to let moisture escape, and let the waning heat do its thing. Just remember to remove your trays before switching the oven on again!

Chapter 3

Food

There are a few things about human existence that remain the same across the globe, and the need to eat food is one of them. Ingredients, amounts, styles, and attitudes towards food vary depending on a range of factors, but the fact that we all need to eat, and that food must be sourced and prepared and any waste associated with it must be taken care of, remains constant.

Because it has so much to do with humans, animals, the environment, and equality, food is a big part of permaculture thinking. Which is great, because we can use the 12 permaculture principles (see page 11) to help guide us and remind us to make better choices.

The internet is full of waste-saving cooking and gardening hacks, and there are plenty more available in books, including this one. But there's a limit to how much we can defer to recipes and written instructions on any given day. So when I'm learning something new, I try to find the Big Picture thinking behind it that resonates with me, and then see how it can slot into my own everyday thinking.

For example, when I decided I wanted to eat more foods with an overall low ecological footprint, I started by considering smaller questions whenever I shopped for food. Where it was made, how the ingredients were farmed, whether it was grown locally and seasonally, and how ecologically sustainable the packaging was all became factors in my selection processes.

Essentially, I try to think about the whole life of any item before I bring it into my living system. Where along its journey has its ecological footprint increased? How much water was used to produce it? Did its production involve chemicals that harm ecosystems? Was there machinery involved and did it use non-renewable energy? How far did it have to travel, and did its transport involve non-renewable fuel? Is it packaged, and is the packaging made in an eco-conscious way? Were the workers involved in its production treated ethically?

Every bit of food we buy, eat or throw away has a history. We may not be able to change that history, but we can make informed decisions in choosing foods that have minimally ecologically harmful histories.

A MEATY TOPIC

The meat vs plant diet debate has been raging for decades, and there's certainly more information available these days about how to be an ethical meat-eater, but the facts of global meat consumption can no longer be denied. If every person in the 38 OECD countries ate meat just one less day per week, the amount of edible grain freed up would be in the hundreds of thousands of tons.

It was the celebrated geobiologist and author Hope Jahren who really got me thinking about how much plants are involved in the people care and fair share ethics of permaculture. In her book *The Story of More*, she talks about how the starvation experienced by thousands of people around the world is not a result of the planet's inability to provide food for all humans, but rather of our reluctance to spread available resources around fairly. If eating more vegetables and less meat was the norm, the potential for reducing global food scarcity would increase dramatically.

Fortunately, there are many plant-based options being produced today, and it's easier than ever to reduce our regular meat intake. Of course there are facets of plant-based food production that could do with improvement from an environmental point of view, but that's where our choice comes into play.

MONEY TALKS

As consumers, we have incredible power to bring about change when we hit at the root of all capitalist production: we can vote with our dollar. Where and on what we choose to spend our money shows food industry players what we're prepared to accept. As always, yes, change via legislation needs to come from the top as well, but the influence we have from the bottom up shouldn't be discounted.

While we're waiting for the food industry to catch up to public demand, it's sometimes necessary to choose between the lesser of two evils. Eggs are a good example: in recent years many people have shifted away from buying caged eggs, which means 'pasture-raised' eggs tend to sell out first in supermarkets. Those of us making a selection from what's left sometimes have to make the best worst choice. Taking 60 seconds to consider which is better out of 'free-range' and 'free range with less than 10,000 hens per m^2' (it's the second, FYI) and voting with our dollars has the power to communicate what we want. Over time, this can change an industry's standards.

Now, because life is busy, most of us don't have the capacity to think deeply about every single interaction with food. Rather than letting that limitation deter us from trying though, it's worth creating a stash of simple ways to make positive eco-swaps on the run.

New thinking becomes habitual only when it's scaffolded, incremental and repeated: if we try to do everything all at once, we burn out and often return to old ways quite quickly. Starting with small, easily achievable changes allows us to build upon our successes, and over time this incremental growth of positive actions can equate to great lifelong habits.

To help me effectively think about the environmental impact of the food I eat, I break things down into little chunks, and work on them one at a time. In permaculture principle terms: I use small and slow solutions. This seems to be how most of my students learn best too.

I broadly lump my ideas into these four categories:

1. How I think about food
2. How I obtain food
3. How I make food last
4. What I do with food.

This chapter contains loads of thoughts and actions to add to your stash under these categories. So choose an area you'd like to work on, read on with your 'pick 'n' mix' basket in hand, and get ready to make some positive change.

How I think about food

MEAL PLANNING

Meal planning can look wildly different for different people. Some use it for budgeting purposes, others for health and fitness reasons, others still because it's the only way they can manage a busy schedule. I think the greatest value of meal planning comes from its ability to make the fullest use of food.

But it doesn't work for everyone. As an anxious, neurospicy person, I can be fairly demand-avoidant when I'm under pressure. That used to lead to me resisting what was on the menu, even if I was the one who wrote it in the first place. Silly, I know, but I accepted the feedback and used it to apply self-regulation. Now, I choose four or five meals I'd like to have in a week, buy the necessary ingredients, and then allow future-Anna to decide what she feels like eating each day. It's led to far less food waste, so I'm chalking it up as an overall win.

Before making a meal plan, 'shop at home' first, by checking what ingredients you already have on hand. Think about the fridge, freezer, pantry and garden. From there, create a rough plan of what you'll eat in the upcoming week, then line up recipes and use them to create a shopping list detailing what you need to source outside the home.

Try to 'stack functions' (see page 12) when it comes to ingredients: plan several meals that use cauliflower so you can buy a whole head (instead of a plastic-wrapped half). That way, you're less likely to end up with a slimy, sad mess in the bottom of the fridge.

Cater appropriately. Think realistically about how much food you actually need for the time ahead. Don't make or plan stuff that won't be eaten, either from a quantity point of view, or because it's not a favourite in the household.

Keeping records of recipes you try or want to try is really useful for meal planning. A scrapbook, a notebook where you jot recipes down, recipe-keeping apps, or online pinboards like Pinterest are good for this.

With all of this said, a lot of the people I look up to don't meal-plan at all. Their cooking style is highly adaptive, and they come up with what to cook on the fly, based on the ingredients they have. In some cases, they use food rescued from the waste stream via 'dumpster diving' or community sharing stands. To get to this stage, though, most of them went through long phases of learning to cook adaptively.

Dumpster diving

Supermarkets throw out hundreds of kilos of food each year, but much of it is still edible, and it's discarded only because of arbitrary 'best before' dates or stock turnover schedules. Dumpster diving is the act of sorting through that 'waste' and reclaiming foods that are still fine to eat. Be sure to check the legality of this waste-busting action in your region before diving in.

ADAPTABLE THINKING

Upskill your cooking capacity. Read books, attend classes, learn from experts in person, on TV or online. Pick a recipe or cuisine to learn more about, and try it out a few times. You could try one new recipe per month from a particular cuisine: by the end of a year, you'll have a better understanding of how that cuisine works, and feel more confident intuitively adapting and substituting ingredients.

Learn to create 'base recipes'. Read multiple recipes for the same dish, identify the ingredients and proportions they have in common, and *bam!* You've got a base recipe! Having this knowledge allows you to be more creative when following recipes. What if a recipe calls for 1 cup of cream but you don't have enough? No worries, other recipes for the same dish use ¾, ½ and 1¼ cups, so obviously that bit is flexible. Proceed with what you've got! That's how I created my recipe for quick jam cake (see page 98), and it's often my starting point when developing new recipes for preserves.

Learn more about foods – where they're from, how to store them, what they taste like, how to use them. This allows you to become more adaptable in your cooking. For example, knowing that zucchini or choko can be substituted for green papaya in a Filipino soup recipe means you can consider using any of those three ingredients in similar dishes too. What if a recipe calls for sour cream but you don't have any? Homemade yoghurt can probably do the job! Start thinking of ingredients as actors: sometimes you need a big star, sometimes the understudy gets to step up.

Versatile veggies

Choko – also known as chayote, chow-chow or mirliton – is an easy, prolific, versatile plant to grow. Sprout a fruit on the windowsill, then in spring plant it half-buried in well-drained soil in part to full sun after the risk of frost has passed. Choko grows as a climbing vine, with masses of fruit, so it needs trellising. All parts of the plant are edible.

Avoid 'single use' foods by buying whole ingredients and unprocessed ingredients, as this allows you to stack their functions. For example, rather than buying single-use sachets of taco or curry seasoning, buy individual spices and learn to make your own seasoning blends. The same goes for sauces and dressings: many of these are super-simple to make using basic ingredients like oils, acids (vinegar, lemon juice), alliums (garlic, onion etc.) and herbs. The cost per serve will almost always work out cheaper this way, it generates less packaging waste, and you can tweak the flavours to suit your taste.

And finally, remember that each meal is just a meal. It's not something you have to present for assessment: no-one's coming along with a clipboard to give you a grade for it. Once it's eaten, it's done. It may not be the best thing you've ever eaten, but you'll be fed, and chances are you'll learn from it, which is all part of improving your knowledge and skills.

How to make yoghurt

Makes 1 litre

There are lots of ways of making yoghurt, but the basics stay the same: heat some milk, cool it back down, add some yoghurt culture, keep it warm for a while. You don't *need* any special equipment, but you can often pick up what's known as a yoghurt maker – essentially just an insulated container in which to keep your yoghurt jar warm as it does its yoghurting transformation – from an op shop for very little, and they can make things much simpler.

Some people use commercial culture to make yoghurt, others use a spoonful of their previous batch or some store-bought pot-set yoghurt. Some keep their jar warm in a drawer filled with blankets and sleeping bags, others favour an insulated esky; it's even possible to use a dehydrator or microwave. You can play around with any sort of milk – cow, goat, fresh, ultra-heat-treated (UHT), even coconut – to make yoghurt, but you may need to adjust the method to find what works best.

INGREDIENTS

1 litre/4 cups dairy milk

1 tbsp pot-set yoghurt or a sachet of commercially made yoghurt culture

METHOD

1   Heat the milk to *almost* boiling in a saucepan over low–medium heat.

Heating milk to 85°C/185°F kills off harmful bacteria (this process is known as pasteurisation) and breaks down (denatures) the milk proteins, which results in a thicker yoghurt. If you don't have a thermometer, watch the milk as it heats up, and as soon as you see steam and frothy bubbles starting to rise, cut the heat.

If you're using UHT milk, you can skip this step, because the milk has already been heated.

You can use milk that is close to its expiry date to make yoghurt: the heating process effectively resets the timeline by killing off bacteria that would cause the yoghurt to spoil.

2   Allow the milk to cool to about 45°C/113°F.

Yoghurt is formed when a culture of specific microorganisms (*Streptococcus thermophilus* and *Lactobacillus delbrueckii* subsp. *bulgaricus*) feed on sugars in the milk to produce lactic acid. This acid gives yoghurt its characteristic tang. These bacteria die off in very hot milk, but thrive between 40°C/104°F and 46°C/115°F, so cool your pasteurised milk to this point before adding the culture.

If you're sans thermometer, dip an ultra-clean finger into the milk. If it's hotter than your body temp, but cool enough to keep your finger in for 30 seconds, you're good to go.

3   Add the yoghurt or yoghurt culture. Stir it in, or leave it as one dollop: either works.

4   Bung it all in a clean jar and seal with a lid.

Pour it all into a very clean jar that will fit into whatever you're going to use to keep it warm. You can reuse a plastic yoghurt pot: just make sure it's been hot-washed with detergent and air-dried. You want to avoid introducing any bacteria or yeasts.

5   Keep the jar warm for 8–24 hours.

Nestle your jar into something to keep it warm for some hours. Try not to disturb it too much while the cultures do their thing. Depending on the conditions, the yoghurt will form within 4–12 hours, and you can leave it fermenting for up to 24 hours. It'll get thicker and tangier the longer you leave it.

6   Store the yoghurt in the refrigerator.

It will keep for several weeks in the fridge.

To transform your yoghurt into labneh, which is a delicious alternative to cream cheese, mix a pinch of salt into 1 litre/4 cups of yoghurt then strain it overnight through a strainer lined with a scalded cloth and placed over a bowl.

How I obtain food

GROWING FOOD

It's been said that growing your own food is the best way to spend six months and hundreds of dollars to produce something that'd cost you $1.39 at the grocer. Others say it's like printing your own money. So which is true? Turns out it can be a bit of both.

It *is* possible to grow all the fresh produce your household needs, even in a suburban property with limited space. Permaculture educator Kat Lavers grew 428 kg/944 lb of produce in a year in her small garden, the Plummery, on just four hours of work per week in 2018. But it's definitely something that requires some thought, planning and self-regulation.

GETTING STARTED

Before you rush out to buy bags of potting mix and punnets of seedlings, take a moment to consider what you want to achieve, and think about your capacity to make that happen. Read up on the time required to manage long-term crops (e.g. asparagus, rhubarb and tree fruit), and assess whether you can commit to that. Explore what's involved in growing from seeds vs from seedlings. If time is scarce, perhaps focus your efforts on short-term or 'cut and come again' crops like leafy greens and herbs. If you have the capacity, crops that grow and produce within one or two seasons, such as tomatoes, cucurbits (cucumbers, pumpkins, zucchini), strawberries, beans, peas and spring onions, are all worth a shot.

Good advice is to grow what you eat, and then actually *eat what you grow*. Avoid the temptation to grow all the pretty things if you're not going to eat them, as this ends up being a waste of time, money and resources. Work out how much you want to harvest, then plant accordingly. Choose varieties to suit your space and requirements: for people with pots or limited space, dwarf and 'heavy-cropping' varieties are often best.

But the very best advice I've ever received was to grow *soil* before anything else. Healthy soil is the foundation of a thriving garden, and you'll get a much better return on your gardening input – both financial and physical – if you get the soil pumping first.

'Grow a Garden'

NO-DIG GARDENING

I avoid commercial soil and potting mix wherever possible, because growing in these mediums creates a cycle of reliance that connects me to plant nurseries. Often this plastic-bagged stuff is little more than chip bark pumped with nutrients that become depleted by plant growth in just a few months, meaning you'll have to either introduce commercial fertilisers or replace it completely every growing season.

My preferred growing medium is no-dig garden beds (also called no-till or 'lasagne' beds). These are popular among permaculture folk because they allow you to repurpose garden and household organic waste into soil, thus creating a circular system.

The English gardening great Charles Dowding has written masses about no-dig growing, and his resources are invaluable if you want to learn more. The basic idea I like to picture with no-dig beds is that they imitate a forest floor. Trees drop dried leaves, passing animals leave behind rich fertiliser, fresh plant matter breaks off in storms and is added to the mix, worms and microorganisms munch through everything, and over time, it all breaks down into a beautiful rich soil.

You can build no-dig gardens on existing soil, on lawn, directly on top of concrete, and even in pots. The ingredients will vary according to the resources you have available, but I like to include autumn leaves collected from my street, pea straw (the only ingredient I buy), worm castings (worm poo from my worm farm, or what's left after they've chowed through my food scraps), homemade compost, shredded paper, prunings, spent plants, and occasionally some small twiggy branches.

Healthy soil grows healthy food

Charles Dowding, author of No Dig *and* Compost, *landowner and large-scale rural grower, @charles_dowding, United Kingdom*

'Growing food for sale has become unprofitable, therefore not many people are doing it, and there are many fewer small farms, small holdings and homesteads where people sell their surplus. That's the kind of food I want, fresh from healthy soil. Healthy soil is key to many good things. My market garden runs at a loss, so I subsidise it from my other work and that enables me to sell super-healthy food. Fortunately, there are still farmers near me who practise traditional methods, and we can still buy eggs, dairy products, and occasionally meat from them.'

PROS AND CONS OF GROWING IN POTS

There will always be benefits to growing in large garden beds, but don't let anyone tell you you can't grow what you like if you're limited to growing in pots. At my rental I have long-term perennials such as rhubarb, fruit trees (my apricot tree has lived in eight different rentals, and one year it produced 3 kg/6½ lb of fruit), native flowering plants, and all manner of leafy greens and summer veggies, all growing in pots I sourced secondhand. And I haven't bought soil or potting mix for over seven years.

Pros

+ Plants can be moved from one house to the next

+ Plants can be shifted as needed (e.g. you can bring your chillies inside in winter to protect them from frosts)

+ Pots are cheap if you source them secondhand

+ Pots are cheap to fill if you use no-dig layers

+ Pots keep pests and pathogens contained, thus reducing their impact across the whole garden.

Cons

+ Pots dry out more quickly than garden beds, so they require more diligent and more frequent mulching and watering

+ Pots can limit the size of plants if you don't pot them up to a larger size as needed

+ Pots provide snails and slugs with hidey-holes.

I've had great success with grouping my pots together to reduce the exposed surface area of the pots, and with adding insulation to the outside of these groups. I also find that using no-dig layers in pots makes them less likely to dry out in summer. And when it comes to the crawling munching beasties, I just go out at night to pull them off my plants and feed them to a neighbour's chooks.

How to grow food in no-dig pots

INGREDIENTS

Lots of carbon-rich material such as pea straw or dried leaves (see page 81 for more examples)

Water

A pot

Compost

Fertiliser such as worm castings or aged chook poo

METHOD

1   Thoroughly saturate the pea straw or dried leaves with water.

2   Create a dense layer of this material in the pot, 10–15 cm/4–6 inches thick. Really pack it in.

3   Add a 5 cm/2 inch layer of compost on top. Water thoroughly.

4   Sprinkle a 10 cm/4 inch layer of fluffy chopped pea straw on top. Water thoroughly.

5   Scatter a sparse layer of fertiliser over the straw, no more than a handful for most pots. Water thoroughly.

6   Repeat steps 3–5 until the pot is almost filled, then finish with a layer of pea straw.

7   To plant in a no-dig pot straight away, scoop out a 'nursery' hole twice the size of the plant's pot or rootball.

8   Cover the base of the hole with sifted compost or potting mix.

9   Position your plant in the centre of the hole. Backfill with sifted compost or potting mix and top with pea straw.

10   Water in well.

By the time the roots have reached the edge of the 'nursery' hole, the no-dig layers around it should have begun breaking down enough to allow for continued root growth.

1

2

3

7

10

MIMICKING NATURE

When it comes to pests in the garden, there's a lot to be said for doing ... nothing. Nature is full of diverse food webs, and there are predators for most pests that affect fruit and veg gardens. The aim in a thriving permaculture living system is to achieve a balanced system in which different elements support each other. When it comes to pests, the sustainable gardener's job is to observe the mini-beasts in their ecosystem and try to help them achieve that balance, which means knowing what different stages of life look like for beneficial bugs so they're not mistaken for pests.

Natural predators are going to turn up in a system only when there's a reliable source of food for them. This means we have to fight the urge to apply chemical pest solutions and allow prey to reach population levels that invite natural predators. Learning the signs that predator help is on the way allows us to hold back from intervening too early. Here are some common garden 'helpers' that might show up, signs that they're hard at work, and the names of pests they feed on.

Beneficial bug – adult	Beneficial bug – young	Pesky prey
Parasitic wasps	Larval cocoons	Cabbage white butterfly caterpillars
Praying mantises	Oothecae (egg capsules)	Aphids, caterpillars, grasshoppers, cabbage moths, cabbage white butterflies, mosquitoes
Lacewings	Eggs	Aphids, mites, thrips
Ladybugs	Nymphs	Aphids, mites, scale, leaf hoppers, mealy bugs

Parasitic wasp

Parasitic wasp larval cocoons

Cabbage white butterfly grubs

Praying mantis

Praying mantis ootheca (egg capsule)

Aphid

Lacewing

Lacewing eggs

Mites

Ladybugs

Ladybug nymphs

Leafhoppers

WHERE YOU CAN GROW

When it comes to choosing areas to use for growing food, bear in mind that different fruit and veg require different minimum amounts of sunlight per day. Leafy veg need at least three hours, rooting crops at least five, and fruiting plants at least seven hours of sunlight per day. Assess your space and map out good growing locations for what you want to plant based on how much sunlight each area gets.

If you have concrete paving or live in a rental that won't allow garden beds, know that you can grow in pots in most situations: more on that on page 82.

more on that on page 82.

Areas where you might not have considered growing food include window boxes (great for herbs from a watering and harvesting perspective), indoor windowsills (microgreens, sprouts, herbs), the bathroom (ginger and turmeric love a steamy tropical environment), a nature strip (check with councils before digging, and prepare for Community interaction), or the dinky bit of soil along a driveway.

You can create vertical growing space by erecting trellises or arbours, or even attaching strings to a fence. Items such as animal hutch netting, mattress springs and even washing-machine drums can all be usefully repurposed in the garden. Consider growing potted climbers like beans, cucumbers and tomatoes outside windows to provide seasonal living shadecloth.

For longer-growing crops such as root veg, alliums (garlic, onions), perennials (asparagus, rhubarb) and fruit trees, in-ground beds or raised beds are great because as they aren't as prone to temperature and water fluctuations as pots.

Weighing up the options
Fabian Capomolla, renter and small-scale suburban grower, @the_hungry_gardener, Australia

'I don't try to be self-sufficient, but I always have something from the garden to add to my meals, even if it's just some herbs. My proudest moment was when I grew veggies in my front yard and on the nature strip. It connected me not only to my garden but to my community. I try to be creative with our meals and make do with what we have in the pantry and garden.

'We have a lot of farmers markets in our area, but I grow a lot of the leafy greens they have on offer. I shop at the local butcher and sometimes order in bulk from a local organic wholesale butcher. I shop at the greengrocer, but their produce isn't locally sourced. Otherwise, I do use supermarkets.

'Sometimes the fact that I'm renting means I don't invest in long-term infrastructure that would make growing food easier and more efficient. It's not always an excuse ... but I do have to weigh it up.'

COMPOST AND WORMS

If you're going to grow some of your own food,
it's also good to consider ways to make your own
compost (see page 221) and worm fertiliser (see
page 212) from food and garden waste.

There are many more ways you can do this than
I can cover in this book, so I recommend checking
out the compost-related Further resources on
page 252 if you'd like to learn more. There's an
option for every living situation, so don't assume
composting is out of reach for you.

WATER

Last, but definitely not least, water is a vital element
to consider carefully when growing your own food.
Plants go into survival mode if they're put under
stress. Lack of consistent watering can lead to
stunted growth, fragile roots, increased susceptibility
to pests and disease, minimal or small fruits and
the development of hydrophobic soil, which leads
to further challenges.

You can promote deeper root growth (and thereby
sturdier plants) by watering less frequently but
ensuring a thorough soaking. I like to water my potted
no-dig garden once a week during spring and maybe
twice a week in the hottest summer months.

If you have limited capacity to water consistently,
you may like to investigate wicking beds or olla
(pronounced OY-ah) pots, which are terracotta
vessels made to be buried in the middle of garden
beds. Both hold a large reservoir of water that will
slowly drain into the soil from below the surface,
encouraging roots to grow deep and strong, but with
less frequent intervention from you. Instructions for
DIY versions are available online.

Other alternatives to consider are drip-line watering
systems and timer-based watering systems. Just be
sure you're still eyeballing your plants at least twice
a week; otherwise, it's easy to miss early signs of
stress or disease.

Olla pot in a garden bed

FORAGING

There's a whole chapter on foraging coming up next, so head there for specifics, but in general, foraged food features as a supplement or enhancement to the food I already make regularly. I keep an eye out for what's growing seasonally, and I choose to make meals that use those things: things like pesto when weedy greens are in abundance, or soup and risotto when edible wild mushrooms are up.

Another type of foraging I like to do, which requires no real new skills or learning, is home foraging. Every four to six weeks, I say to myself, 'Right! I'm not allowed to buy anything new this week except milk and bread. Everything else *has* to come from the fridge, freezer, pantry or garden!'

Learning to create a meal from limited ingredients may sound daunting, but it's actually quite fun when you get stuck in. There are lots of websites and apps out there (SuperCook, RecipeRadar, MyFridgeFood) designed to spit out recipes based on the ingredients you have. More often than not, I get to the end of my home foraging week and I haven't had a chance to try out some of the recipes I wanted to, so I end up pushing it out a little bit further. Over time, this reduces lots of waste, and saves me money too.

Small steps in suburbia
Kathryn Jackson, suburban homeowner and occasional grower, Australia

'I have a super-busy life as a business owner and mum of two, so time is my scarcest resource. I used to grow a fair bit of food: these days that's not feasible, but I do grow herbs and some leafy greens during summer. I sometimes get to shop at a farmers market, but otherwise, I rely on greengrocers and the supermarket for my fresh produce. I try to stick to what's in season and will always pick Aussie-grown when I can. I've been buying more dry goods like nuts, rice and flour from my local bulk-food store too, and I love that it's organic and packaging-free.'

SOURCING WELL

Given how much of our food's carbon footprint comes from the processes used to grow, store and transport it, doing your best to make informed, conscious decisions on where you source your food from is a really powerful action to take in the war against waste.

The produce we see in supermarkets is *heavily* curated. Strict industry standards for the shape, size and appearance of fresh produce mean that staggering percentages of fresh food are dumped as waste before they even reach the shelves. Some of these specifications are designed to reduce the amount of diseased or damaged fruit that leaves producers' facilities, but many are cosmetic – things like 'That cherry is the wrong shade of red' or 'That apple is too large'. The most ridiculous one I've seen is 'That banana isn't curved enough'.

Some supermarkets stock 'ugly' fruit and veg, but these often come with extra packaging, and they aren't much cheaper even though the farmers who grew them have been paid less for them. An awesome alternative is signing up to receive a fruit and veg delivery box from a company that sources 'ugly' produce directly from farmers. Not only do these services shorten supply chains and reduce waste for farmers, but they save you money (being cheaper than supermarket produce) and encourage you to cultivate your seasonal and creative cooking skills.

10 ways to source your food 'well'

+ Buy from greengrocers, where you can have a say in the produce you'd like to see stocked, rather than supermarkets

+ Shop at farmers markets

+ Buy directly from farmers at farmgate stalls or online

+ Buy from bulk-food stores

+ Buy only seasonal produce

+ Buy only produce sourced from your own country or region

+ Rescue less-than-perfect produce from the 'use it or lose it' table

+ Go 'dumpster diving' (see page 74)

+ Donate to and take from community sharing stands (see page 35)

+ Become part of a food co-op.

Buying in bulk and choosing 'nude food' or recyclable paper, glass or metal packaging are some ways to reduce the overall carbon footprint of your food. For more on food packaging, see page 208.

MAKING YOUR OWN

As the cost of living increases, many foods that used to make it into the shopping basket regularly may start to seem like expensive luxuries. Non-essentials like sweets, biscuits and crackers quickly shift into this category, but things like cheese, yoghurt and cereals aren't far behind.

Learning to make some of these foods from scratch may feel daunting, but truly, there are so many recipes available these days that it's likely to be much simpler than you imagine. Making my own yoghurt (see page 76) is one of the easiest things I started doing in an effort to be less reliant on supermarkets.

Have a go at making delicious granola or other cereals from ingredients bought at bulk-food stores. Mix biscuit (cookie) dough in bulk then freeze it in batches for quick weekly bakes. Make crackers and naan, pizza dough and pasta with little more than flour, water, oil and a bit of salt – they're cultural staples because they're cheap and easy to make. Whip up fruit leather straps with just fruit and sunshine. Have a crack at sourdough bread. Every swap is a step towards less plastic packaging in the environment, and more pennies in your pocket.

Where do you source your food?

'I grow most of what we eat, including fruit, veg, eggs and some meat. I facilitate large bulk buys of dry goods for my community. I began a CSA (community-supported agriculture scheme) many years ago which got people growing their own through working bees at the farm. I never shop at a supermarket.' – Su

Quick jam cake

Makes 1 large loaf tin

'Quick', 'jam' and 'cake' are words that make many people happy. This combo of all three makes use of basic ingredients, very little effort, and just ten minutes of active work to produce a delicious moist, jammy cake that never fails to bring smiles to the table. It's perfect made with homemade jam (see page 160) and homemade yoghurt (see page 76), but use any sweet preserve you have on hand: it's just the thing for using up those mostly empty jars lingering in the fridge.

No jam? Just plop in some berries (fresh, frozen or dried) or pieces of fresh fruit.

INGREDIENTS

1 cup pot-set yoghurt

2 eggs

⅓ cup neutral oil (canola, sunflower etc.)

⅓–½ cup sugar

2 cups self-raising flour

Some jam – ½ cup or a bit more

METHOD

1   Preheat the oven to 180°C/375°F fan-forced (200°C/400°F convection).

2   Line a large loaf tin with compostable baking paper.

3   Mix the yoghurt, egg and oil in a bowl with a fork until smooth and combined.

4   Add the sugar and flour and stir until combined.

5   Spoon half the mixture evenly into the prepared tin. Dollop the jam over the top. Spoon the remaining mixture over the jam and smooth the surface.

6   Bake for 30–40 minutes or until a skewer inserted into the centre comes out clean.

How I make food last

Food decomposes when naturally occurring microorganisms (bacteria, mould etc.) feed on it. These microorganisms need moisture, oxygen and heat to thrive, so storing food in airtight containers in a cold place deprives them of their needs, thus slowing decomposition. There are lots of different storage options available. Let's look at what works best and is environmentally sound.

FRIDGE

Plates Use to store fruit and veg with just one cut surface, or use as covers on top of bowls, cups, dishes etc., in lieu of plastic wrap.

Used plastic bags If you've got'em, use'em! Good for storing root veg.

Plastic containers The seals are often imperfect, so they're not necessarily good for long-term storage. Use them for leftovers, prepped cooking ingredients, veggie sticks for a party etc.

Glass jars My favourite! Airtight seals keep food fresh the longest. Great for berries, grapes, all vegetables and fruits with more than one cut surface, cheese, cured meats, leftovers, smoothies, juice, salads, puddings, pastes ...

Beeswax wraps Good for small and large items. Half a cut cucumber, a lasagne or a quiche – that kind of thing. To make your own, see the instructions on page 209.

Cloth Wrap damp tea towels (dish towels) around leafy greens (herbs, spring onions, celery etc.) and pop them in the crisper to keep them fresh for a week or more.

FREEZER

Ice-cube trays Large or small, these work well for liquids (coconut milk, stock, lemon juice, sauces, smoothies), pastes (tomato, curry) and solids (cooked rice, leftover curry, soup). Once frozen solid, pop the cubes into containers or bags and return them to the freezer.

Glass jars That's right! Provided you don't fill them more than three-quarters full, they won't break. Great for leftovers, drinks, grated ginger and garlic frozen in ice-cube trays, chopped herbs and chillies. Defrost slowly or the jars *will* shatter.

Plastic containers These work well for slices of meat, pre-made patties, slices of cake etc. (separate the layers with baking paper), leftovers, food frozen in ice-cube trays, and chopped fruit.

Where do you source your food?

'Our proteins come mainly from the supermarket, and almost all of our veggies from our suburban garden. Our fruit trees aren't at their maturity yet so we source some fruit from shops seasonally too.' – Connie

PANTRY AND BENCH

Glass jars You'll never convince me reused glass jars aren't the greatest storage containers around. I use them for pretty much everything in the pantry. Collect different sizes from friends, op shops and Community cupboards, and label them with paint markers or paper labels. Use mini-shelves and turntables inside your pantry so jars don't get lost and forgotten at the back.

Ceramic crocks Keep onions and potatoes cool in a ceramic crock, separate from other foods. Ceramics are also good for storing bread, rice, dried beans and pasta.

Vases, jars and crocks Filled with water, these can be used to keep any stemmed, leafy or floral veg crisp for a week or more, in the same way you'd preserve a bunch of flowers. Works well for celery, spring onions, kale, herbs, asparagus and broccoli.

Where do you source your food?

'I can't grow food, largely because I don't have the time or knowledge, but I hate the idea of my food coming from miles away. So I make sure to check the origin of fresh produce and choose locally grown stuff wherever possible. It's not much, but supporting local growers and reducing my carbon footprint feels like an important step towards living more sustainably'. – Dom

Tricky sticky labels

To remove sticky labels from jars, fill them with boiling water and wait for the heat to loosen the adhesive. Rub with oil to remove sticky residue, then wash with hot soapy water and rinse well.

PRESERVATION METHODS RATED AND REVIEWED

With all the energy that goes into growing, harvesting and transporting fresh food, it's worth learning a few different ways to store it to enjoy year round. Preserving is an excellent way of catching the embodied energy in produce when it's seasonally abundant. This allows you to capture food when its flavour, quality and nutritional content are at their peak and store it for enjoyment in times of scarcity – for example, when it's out of season.

People have been eating food since well before electric refrigeration came along, so there are countless inventive ways to preserve food, many of which are very easy to learn. Because there are so many, it's impossible to go into detail on all of them here, but I've published several detailed guides to preserving at theurbannanna.com to help you upskill.

To whet your appetite, here's a snapshot of eight ways to preserve food, including the pros and cons of each method.

I've indicated the time and energy required and the overall difficulty for each method. If something's going to take lots of energy, effort and time to preserve, I question whether it's worth doing. I'll usually do a kind of cost–benefit assessment of different methods and use that to determine which one to use.

KEY:

🕐   Time input

⚡   Energy input

😊   Difficulty rating

Freezing

+ Used to preserve

Raw and cooked meat, veg, fruit, liquids, leftover cooked meals, bread, spices, flavouring ingredients (ginger, garlic, chilli, herbs), veg scraps for making stock.

+ Special equipment

Freezer (usually powered by electricity), reused glass jars, plastic containers, plastic bags, permanent marker and tape for labelling, ice-cube trays for freezing liquids and pastes.

+ Pros

Simple, quick, adaptable. Allows quick capture of embodied energy in times of abundance (e.g. foraged fruit) that can be transformed at a later date in many ways.

+ Cons

Out of sight, out of mind – things often get lost in the glaciers up the back. Requires constant electrical energy. Food is vulnerable to spoilage during power outages.

Dehydrating

+ Used to preserve

Fruits, veggies, flowers, herbs, meat, fish, dairy foods, cooked meals. Can produce meal kits, spice blends, fruit leather and sweets, snacks, food to take hiking, granola, herbal teas, baked goods, dukkah, and bath and body products.

+ Special equipment

Dehydrator, flat baskets or other drying racks.

+ Pros

Low-tech. Some fully dried foods last indefinitely. Energy input is relatively low (lowest if you use passive energy; see page 64). The process shrinks food so storage takes less space. Highly versatile in what can be dried, so it lends itself to creativity.

+ Cons

Preparing ingredients can be time-consuming. Passive drying requires consistent low-level engagement over several days. Nutrients and flavour can be affected by drying temperatures.

Jamming, jellying and marmalade-ing

+ Used to preserve

Fruits of all kinds, and some vegetables.

+ Special equipment

Acid-proof jar lids, and an oven, dishwasher or microwave to sterilise jars. A jam funnel is useful. Otherwise, regular kitchen equipment is fine.

+ Pros

Very long shelf life, familiar flavours (similar to supermarket foods), a very adaptable process, and a delicious way of dealing with seasonal fruit gluts. Excellent gifts.

+ Cons

The process is high in sugar and requires knowledge of sterile handling. High altitude can affect the safety of jar seals, and dented lids or compromised seals can lead to spoilage.

Chutney-ing and relishing

+ Used to preserve

Fruit and veg, especially when they're in abundance.

+ Special equipment

Acid-proof jar lids, and an oven, dishwasher or microwave to sterilise jars. A jam funnel is useful. Otherwise, regular kitchen equipment is fine.

+ Pros

Very long shelf-life, familiar flavours (similar to supermarket foods), a very adaptable process, and the products get better with age. Excellent gifts.

+ Cons

Often includes lots of onions, garlic and high-fructose ingredients, so less suitable for people following some low-FODMAP diets. Requires knowledge of sterile handling. Longer cooking times than sweet preserves. High altitude can affect the safety of jar seals, and dented lids or compromised seals can lead to spoilage.

Pickling

+ Used to preserve

Fruit and veg (can be used to make pickled fish and meats too, although this is less common).

+ Special equipment

Acid-proof lids, and an oven, dishwasher or microwave to sterilise jars. A jam funnel is useful. Otherwise, regular kitchen equipment is fine.

+ Pros

Pickles have a very long shelf life. The flavours are familiar (similar to supermarket foods). The process is very adaptable.

+ Cons

Requires thorough knowledge of food acidity and sterile handling. High altitude can affect the safety of jar seals, and dented lids or compromised seals can lead to harmful spoilage.

Quickling (quick pickling)

+ Used to preserve

All the things you'd otherwise pickle slowly.

+ Special equipment

Nil. Reused jars and regular cookware are fine.

+ Pros

So easy! Works for all the fruit and veg you might pickle using other methods, and ready within one or two days. Delicious sweet and tangy results.

+ Cons

Quick pickles have a shorter shelf life than fully preserved pickles. Must be refrigerated.

Bottling and hot-water-bath canning

+ Used to preserve

Fruit – whole or in pieces – and some high-acid vegetables (e.g. tomatoes).

+ Special equipment

Special jars, lids and seals (e.g. Ball Mason or Fowler's Vacola) or regular reused glass jars with lids that seal well. A Fowler's Vacola unit or large pot in which to process jars. The equipment can be expensive, but almost everything is reusable again and again.

+ Pros

This method produces food similar to tinned food, and it's easy to use in recipes. You can add as much or as little sugar as you like, and the process involves no preservatives (although you may need to add some lemon juice or citric acid to low-acid fruits). Makes you feel like a proper 'homesteader'.

+ Cons

It can be costly to gather the necessary equipment. The process requires thorough, specific knowledge, as errors can lead to harmful spoiled food. Altitude can affect the safety of jar seals and processing times must be calculated accurately.

Fermenting

+ Used to preserve

Fruits, veg, dairy. Makes pickles, kimchi, sauerkraut, kvass, kefir, kombucha, vinegar, yoghurt, wild soda, beer, cider, wine, miso, tempeh and soy sauce.

+ Special equipment

This depends on the type of fermenting you want to do. Specialist fermenting crocks can be useful, but most lacto-fermenting can be done with simple reused jars.

+ Pros

Fermentation is one of the safest preserving methods – very little can go seriously wrong. It's low-tech yet produces foods high in nutrients and full of good gut bacteria. Requires very little active involvement. Incredible soured and umami flavours are possible from the simplest ingredients.

+ Cons

Some willingness to make mistakes is necessary: you will have some dud batches (but they're great for learning!).

HOW TO LACTO-FERMENT

'Kimchi'

Lacto-fermentation has had a resurgence in popularity recently, and with good reason. It allows you to preserve nutritious food when it's seasonally abundant for enjoyment when times are more lean; it's cheap and simple to do, requiring very little specialist equipment; and the food produced is teeming with beneficial bacteria to promote increased gut health.

Fermenting – in particular lacto-fermenting – is one of the safest methods of preserving food, and it has been done for centuries in the most basic of conditions. Once a food is fermented and then chilled, it can technically remain safe to eat for years. It will continue fermenting very slowly even in the refrigerator, so generally the texture and flavour will be best if enjoyed within six to 12 months.

At its most basic, lacto-fermenting involves surrounding fresh fruit, veg or herbs with brine (salty water), which kills off harmful bacteria while letting naturally occurring *Lactobacillus* bacteria convert the food sugars into lactic acid and carbon dioxide. The gas causes bubbles (that's why fermented food often fizzes), and the lactic acid preserves the food in a similar way to vinegar.

Lacto-fermentation doesn't involve any dairy products! It gets its name from the *Lactobacillus* bacteria that transform fresh ingredients into tangy preserved delights.

To get you started on your fermenting journey, here's a set of recipes that cover three different methods of lacto-fermenting:

1   Massaging the main ingredients with a salty paste to produce a brine (scrap-chi, or scraptastic kimchi, see page 118)

2   Adding salt to the main ingredients and allowing pressure and time to draw out their liquid to form a brine (summer salsa, see page 121)

3   Adding a premixed brine to firm ingredients that won't release much liquid during fermentation (cheat's dill pickles, see page 122).

With each recipe, you can experiment with using whatever vegetables you have, but make sure you use salt that's free from any additives. 'Pickling' salt, kosher salt, sea salt, lake salt – all are suitable.

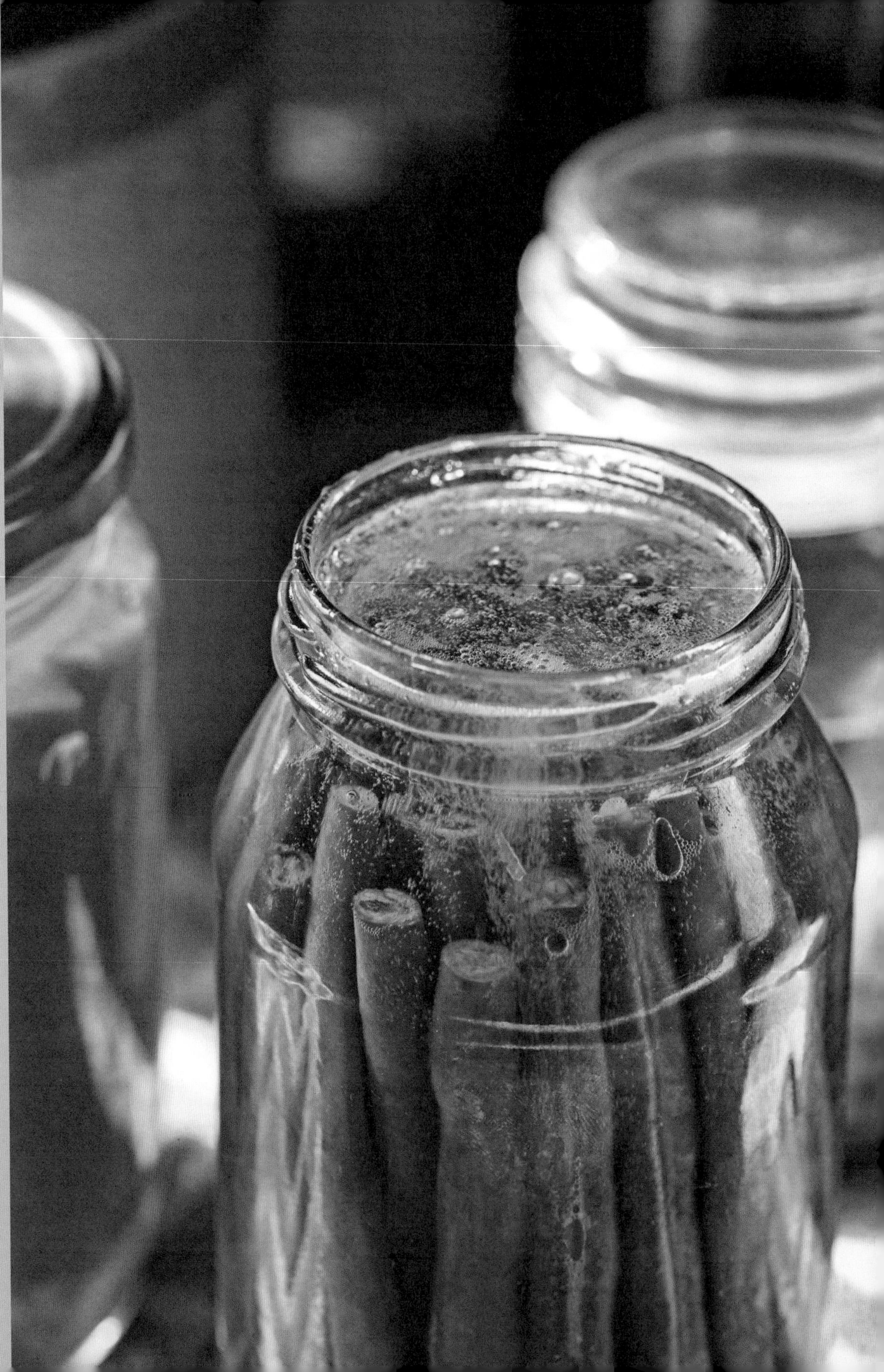

HOW TO CALCULATE 3% SALT

Most recipes for fermented foods ask you to calculate the weight of salt required as a percentage of the weight of the main ingredients, or to make a brine solution that is a certain salinity (saltiness). The purpose is to make sure there's enough salt in the mix to kill off harmful bacteria, but not so much that it prevents *Lactobacillus* bacteria from doing their job. The calculation often looks confusing and overly technical in print, but in real life, and with a set of digital scales, it's much easier than it looks.

Typically, 2–3% salinity is enough to kill off most undesirable bacteria.* This is infinitely easier to calculate in metric terms ('per cent' means 'per 100') than in imperial measurements, so get yourself some digital scales that can measure grams if you're keen to get into fermenting.

Let's say you've got a recipe that calls for 100 g of veggies and 3% of their weight in salt. To calculate 3% of 100 g calculate 0.03 x 100. This equals 3, so you add 3 grams of salt to the 100 grams of veg.

The scrap-chi recipe on page 118 calls for 1 kg of veg and 3% salt.

1 kg = 1000 grams

1000 x 0.03 = 30

= 30 grams of salt for 1 kg of veg.

* I normally use 2% salt, but to help reassure you on the food safety front as you're learning, I've suggested 3% in this book. If your finished ferments are saltier than you like, you can rinse or dilute them with a bit of fresh water just before eating.

Scrap-chi (scraptastic kimchi)

Makes about 1 kg/2 lb 3 oz

This Korean-inspired ferment is a great way to use up odds and sods from the fridge. You'll need a large clean glass jar, plus a slightly smaller jar that fits inside the top, to act as a weight. The quantities here are loose, but you should stick more or less to these ratios.

Enjoy it as a side, in savoury pancakes, as dumpling filling or in a spicy beef soup.

INGREDIENTS

About 1 kg/2 lb 3 oz vegetables. Include some root vegetables (e.g. carrot, turnip, daikon, radish), some brassicas (e.g. wombok, cabbage, broccoli, especially the stems) and some alliums (e.g. onion, shallot, spring onion, wild onion grass)

1 apple, pear or nashi

1 head garlic

1 knob ginger

2 tbsp gochugaru (Korean chilli flakes) or gochujang (Korean chilli paste)

1 tbsp fish sauce or vegan fish sauce (optional)

Salt

METHOD

1   Peel and trim the veggies. Thinly slice the alliums and chop everything else into matchsticks. Combine all the veg in a bowl.

2   Peel and core the apple. Finely slice half of it and grate the other half. Add to the veggies.

3   Mince or crush the garlic and ginger and add to the veggies.

4   Weigh the combined veggies and calculate the amount of salt you will need (see page 117), based on 3% of the weight of the veg.

5   Add the gochugaru or gochujang, fish sauce (if using) and salt to the veggies.

6   Mix everything together, and massage with your hands until a bit of juice (brine) forms at the bottom of the bowl.

7   Firmly pack the mixture, including the brine, into a large, clean jar. Push the smaller clean jar inside the large one so it weighs down the veg. Fill the smaller jar with water to add weight if necessary.

8   Loosely cover everything and leave it on the bench. Overnight, more brine will form, covering the veg.

9   Taste after three or four days. It should taste rich and robust: spicy, garlicky and gingery, with a complex umami-boosted tanginess. If you like it more sour, leave it to ferment for longer. Once it's fermented to your liking, remove the small jar, seal the large jar and refrigerate.

Summer salsa

Perfect for Taco Tuesday, this sassy salsa uses whatever summer veg you've got happening. You'll need a clean glass jar, plus a slightly smaller jar that fits inside the top, to act as a weight.

INGREDIENTS

A mix of summery salsa ingredients – e.g. tomatoes, chillies (start with 1–2, and add more if you like extra heat), garlic, corn, capsicum, cucumber, onion

Salt

Lemon or lime juice (optional)

METHOD

1   Chop all the veg into similar sized pieces: small or large, it's up to you.

2   Weigh the combined veg and calculate the amount of salt you will need (see page 117), based on 3% of the weight of the veg.

3   Add the salt and a squeeze of lemon or lime juice (optional) for extra zing.

4   Mix well, then pack into a clean glass jar.

5   Push the smaller clean jar inside the larger one so it weighs down the veg. Fill the smaller jar with water to add weight if necessary.

6   Loosely cover everything and leave it on the bench. Overnight, brine will form, covering the veg.

7   Taste after two days. It should taste like a fresh, zippy sweet-and-sour salsa, perfect to serve with Mexican dishes or chips and crackers. If you like it more sour, leave it for longer. Once it's fermented to your liking, remove the small jar, seal the larger jar and refrigerate.

Cheat's dill pickles

'Dill pickles' are traditionally made from gherkins or cucumbers, but making them can be challenging to master, and you can easily end up with soggy cukes that turn to mush when handled. This method uses the same method as traditional dill pickles, but it but sidesteps the soggy result by using firm, crisp vegetables instead of cucumbers. It involves adding a premixed brine to firm ingredients that don't release much liquid during fermentation.

INGREDIENTS

Salt

Fresh, firm veg – e.g. green beans, carrots, radishes, onions, spring onion stems

Dill stalks

Garlic

METHOD

1   Make a 3% brine by dissolving 30 g/1 oz salt in 1 litre/4 cups boiling water. Cool to room temperature.

2   Wash and peel the veg, and slice them into roughly equal size sticks that are 5 cm/2 inches shorter than your jar.

3   Tie a couple of dill stalks into a loose knot. Place them in the jar along with 1 crushed garlic clove.

4   Tightly pack the veg into the jar. Really shove them in: you should hear them squeak as they go in.

5   Completely cover the veg with cooled brine. Ensure they're fully submerged.

6   Seal and leave on the bench for three to five days. 'Burp' the jar every day (remove the lid to release carbon dioxide, then put the lid on again).

7   Once the brine is cloudy and bubbly, taste the vegetables. They should taste like a cross between whatever veg you've used and regular dill pickles: tangy, fresh, dilly and slightly sour. If you like them more sour, leave them fermenting for longer. Once they're fermented to your liking, refrigerate.

What I do with food

If food waste were a country, it would be the third largest producer of CO_2 emissions in the world. In Australia, the average household throws away around $2,500 worth of food every year: the equivalent of one in every five bags of groceries ends up in landfill, producing harmful emissions.

The frustrating thing about this – aside from the whole 'harming the ecosystem we rely on' thing – is that there's actually very little of most fresh ingredients that can't be used in one way or another. We've just been conditioned to think otherwise so we'll spend more money at supermarkets.

The first step to reducing waste is getting to know your food better. How long does it stay fresh? Which bits are edible? What do different bits taste like? How can I store them most effectively? How can they be used?

'Best before' dates are being reconsidered in many countries in a bid to reduce food waste. Unlike 'Use by' dates which specify when foods will spoil, 'Best before' dates indicate when foods will begin to 'lose quality'. This might mean flavours will change, or textures will deteriorate, but it doesn't mean you shouldn't eat a food past that date.

When I'm assessing whether to eat a food that seems a bit iffy, I ask myself:

+ Does it have a use-by date or a best-before date?

+ Is it past that date?

+ Does it still look, smell and taste fine?

+ Does it have any really manky bits on it, or is it just looking a bit tired and wibbly?

+ Can I remove some bits to access bits that seem fine to eat?

+ Has it been preserved with sugar, vinegar or a fermentation process? (If it has, it might still be safe to eat even if it's past its use-by date.)

+ Will I be cooking it at high heat before I eat it? (Extended high heat kills a lot of unwanted bacteria.)

+ Do I have any major health and safety concerns about eating this food past its use-by date?

If I doubt my judgement, I use websites such as doesitgobad.com to help make a decision. But I've learned some useful principles that have all helped me to dramatically cut down on food waste:

+ If it's a fermented food, or has heaps of sugar in it, it takes a *lot* for food to 'go bad'.

+ Use-by dates are usually one or two days on the conservative side, so some items may be okay to eat past that date (usually not meat, though).

+ As long as there's no mould growing on it, wibbly and mushy fruit and veg can usually be turned into something fine to eat.

Making considered choices
Kat Nyitray, suburban homeowner, Australia

'I work full time, run a household of five (six if you include the cat) and live a very active life. I only have time to shop once a week, at one place, and I need to keep to a strict budget. Making sustainable and ethical choices is important to us as a family but this needs to be achievable when shopping. So I buy Australian made where I can, avoid single-use plastic and excessive packaging, and try to stick to foods with whole minimal ingredients that are sustainably farmed.

'I like to make as much as possible from scratch to avoid pre-packaged and manufactured foods as cooking is my passion. It's a great way of sharing with my children the importance of not only making sustainable choices but also slowing life down.'

THE APPEAL OF PEEL

Many fruits and most vegetables have peels that are edible and full of flavour (and nutrients!), but just don't have a nice mouthfeel. Check whether there's some way of extracting that flavour. Here are a few of my favourite ways to use up all those edges and margins.

Stock is super-simple to make with veggie, herb and meat scraps (head to page 214 for details).

Cordials and syrups can be used over yoghurt, pancakes and cakes, or diluted with water and enjoyed as a super-flavoursome beverage. Combine strawberry tops, mango pips and peels, or pineapple skins with sugar in a jar. Leave overnight, then strain out the solids.

Tepache is the famous fizzy Mexican beverage made with pineapple skins and cores, but you can follow the same method with most fruit scraps to make wild-fermented sodas. Add the scraps to a jar with some sugar or honey, fill with water, and allow to ferment on the bench for a few days. Strain and serve with ice.

Vinegar can be made from the peels and cores of persimmons, kiwi fruit and apples. Search online for 'fruit vinegar recipes'.

Fruit leather is a tasty low-wastey lunchbox treat. Wash your leftover mango, peach, apple, kiwi, banana, plum or mandarin skins, then boil them with a bit of water and sugar (to taste) until they're soft. Blend to a paste in a food processor and spread out on baking paper. Dehydrate until leathery (see pages 64–66).

Seasoning blends and spice rubs add flavour to roasts, soups and stews. Start by dehydrating veggie peels (tomato is my favourite) then grind the peel to a powder. Add it to creative seasoning blends and spice mixes.

SCRAPTASTIC FOOD

Having a bunch of ideas on hand to use up 'scraps' is the first step to reducing waste. Here are three common ingredients and some of the ways you can use every part of them, from nose to tail, as it were.

Spring onions

Green parts

+ Sandwiches
+ Salads
+ With eggs, avo or cheese on toast
+ Fermented – in kimchi or sauerkraut
+ Chopped and dried
+ Fermented and dried (seaweed substitute)
+ Ramen
+ Fried rice
+ Fritters
+ Pakoras

White parts

+ Pickled or 'quickled' (quick pickled)
+ Fermented with other veg
+ Sautéed as a side
+ Chopped and dried
+ Re-sprouted in water or planted to regrow

Roots

+ Stocks
+ Finely chopped and added to sauces
+ Dried and ground
+ Fried as a crispy snack

Scraps

+ Stocks
+ Soups
+ Dried and added to rubs or salt for seasoning

Celery

Leaves
+ Salad greens
+ Smoothies
+ Pesto
+ Soups
+ Dips
+ Stocks
+ Dried and ground for seasoning

Stalks
+ Snacks
+ Coleslaw
+ Waldorf salad
+ Sauerkraut
+ Stews
+ Sandwich fillings
+ Stir-fries
+ Dipping sticks
+ Sautéed with butter (inner ribs)
+ Juices
+ Bloody Marys

Base
+ Washed, chopped and added to soups
+ Planted and regrown
+ Stocks

Scraps
+ Dried and ground for seasoning
+ Sandwiches
+ Chopped salads

Apples

Peel
+ Chopped and dried for tea
+ Made into vinegar – for dressing, fire cider, surface cleaner, hair conditioner
+ Stocks and soups
+ Wild-fermented soda
+ Pet food – for chooks, rabbits, birds, goats
+ Added to compost or worm farm

Flesh
+ Eat
+ Juice
+ Cider
+ Jam
+ Chutney
+ Apple sauce
+ Baked – pies, cakes, muffins
+ Dried – snacks, tea, granola
+ Fruit leather
+ Stews
+ Soups
+ Fermented – in kimchi, sauerkraut or hot sauce

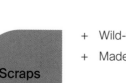

Scraps
+ Wild-fermented soda
+ Made into vinegar

THE SCRAPTASTIC CHALLENGE

Learn to use up food that looks a bit preloved or wibbly, reimagine leftovers as new meals, and use bits of ingredients you wouldn't normally. Turn bottom-of-the-fridge veg into a quiche, pureed soup or fritters once a week. Convert leftover stew into pie filling. Transform cooked spaghetti into a use-it-up pasta bake. Fill toasted sandwiches with bolognese sauce. Make incredible umami dust by grinding dried mushroom stalks.

As for fruit, wash and freeze whole leftover berries until there are enough to make a smoothie. Convert the bowl of apples your toddler has taken one bite out of into a delicious crumble or muffins that they'll devour. Make a fermented side dish like scrap-chi (see page 118). Dry small pieces of sad fruit from the fruit bowl to use in tea blends or granola.

There are *so* many ways to creatively use bits and bobs of food; try setting yourself a challenge where you don't discard anything for a week without stopping to consider whether it could be used in a different way first. You'll be surprised how often you can make something delicious from it, and you may just discover a new family favourite while you're at it!

MANAGING WASTE

Food waste contributes significantly to household waste, and so does food packaging. The best way to reduce it is obviously to avoid bringing it into the household in the first place, but then it's up to you to look for management solutions that keep it out of landfill. There are heaps of ways to reuse or transform waste these days once it does occur, so you just need to figure out which ones work best for you, and then create a clear and simple sorting system to match, which we'll explore in Chapter 5: Waste.

Chapter 4

Foraging

The concept of foraging has been found in anthropological records going back as far as 2 million years. Long after humans largely adopted subsistence farming and modern agriculture, foraging is still a regular part of life for many today.

'Eatin' Weeds'

The idea of urban foraging is to look for edible foods growing in public spaces in urban settings. Y'know, things growing in those marginal spaces that don't seem to be used for much, like laneways or empty house blocks. Sometimes it'll be fruit overhanging footpaths, other times it's trees on nature strips or bushes in public parks.

However it looks, foraging is a way to connect deeply with the land and our food, which in turn can make us grateful for and respectful of our place in the food web. It is steeped in the foundational ethics of permaculture: Earth care, people care, and fair share. But for foraging to be a safe, enjoyable, ethical, and above all sustainable part of life for a broader community, there need to be some self-moderated, self-imposed guidelines in place.

A note on foraging safety

While the author and publisher have made every effort to provide enough information to keep readers safe when identifying plants using this book, the final decision on whether any wild food is safe to eat rests with the individual. Hardie Grant and The Urban Nanna are not responsible for any adverse reactions readers may experience as a result of eating any wild food.

If you suspect you have eaten something poisonous, call the poisons information line in your country:

+ Australia: Poisons Information Centre, 131 126

+ United Kingdom: National Health Service, non-emergencies 111, emergencies 999

+ United States: Poison Control, 1800 222 1222

Grow a brighter future
Lisen Sundgren, lifebylisen.com, Sweden

'[It won't be] sustainable for all of us 9 billion people to go out and forage – we need to find sustainable ways to grow [food]. Education is a big one. [And encouraging] farmers and people with gardens to grow more wild food.'

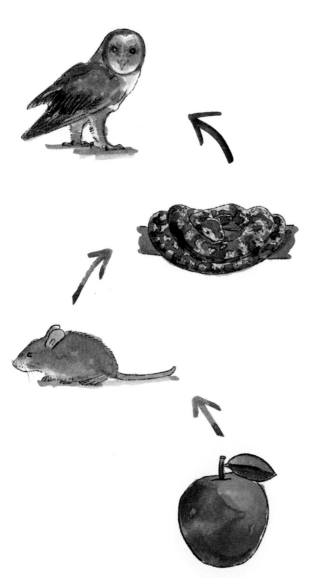

The ethics of foraging

As part of living by permaculture ethics (see page 10), it's vital that we don't upset established balances by indiscriminately picking food wherever we find it. Regardless of whether it's growing wild or you've grown it yourself, 'applying self-regulation' when 'obtaining a yield' should be the standard, otherwise it's too easy to head in the direction of excess and waste.

This means that when harvesting any food, it's good to consider that food's role in its ecosystem and where its value lies – not just its value to you, but its value to other animals and plants. It means asking questions like 'What wildlife relies on this plant for food?', 'Is this food part of a breeding pattern for wildlife, and therefore important to a broad food-web?', and 'What sorts of external factors influence its growth, and do they make it unsafe for me to eat?'.

How can we know the answers to these questions? The truth is, we can't: we can only make an educated guess. We can increase our chances of making a *good* guess by spending time getting to know the area. I spend a year, on average, getting to know a potential foraging spot before taking any kind of yield from it. I observe weather patterns, seasonal wildlife behaviours, fluctuations in crop size, overall plant health, evidence of human interaction, and evidence of contamination with chemicals and other pollutants. All these things help me build a picture of the plant as part of an ecosystem, and allow me to make much more informed decisions on whether I choose to forage in the area, and how.

Slow down and think big

The first step of ethical foraging, in my mind, is to slow down and remember that I'm just one small person in a world-sized bigger picture. I acknowledge the Country I'm on, pay my respects to the First Nations Elders past and present, and consider how I can ensure the land will be taken care of for future Elders. Considering myself as part of a story that began long before me, and will extend far beyond my presence, is an excellent way to remember that I have a place on and a responsibility to our planet. Thinking this way reminds me to tread lightly and leave as little trace of my passing as possible.

Acknowledging my part in a bigger ecosystem entails things like not completely stripping plants of fruits and seeds, and not leaving behind any rubbish. But it also makes me consider things like not breaking branches to access fruit (so as not to damage the parent plant), and not clomping heavily around the area (which compacts soil and damages spaces where biodiversity flourishes).

This is all especially applicable to rural foraging settings, which I know aren't available to everyone. In urban settings, ethical foraging is more about respecting ecosystems that exist between humans. When people are bunched together like they are in urban and suburban spaces, gardens growing abundant produce stick out as an attraction to many, but there are rules and certain social etiquette to follow.

Laws and limits

Most countries have various laws about where it's permissible to pick plant material. In Australia, for example, it's illegal to forage native plants in most states unless you have a licence or the permission of the landholder. Rules on introduced species tend to be less stringent, but there are still laws to limit the spread of invasive plants, pests or disease.

Unwritten rules about what's socially acceptable to forage apply as well. In some places, people say that if the base of the plant is within a property boundary, all fruit is considered off-limits to outsiders. Others say branches overhanging fence lines onto common ground are fair game for all. Among permie foragers, there's an understanding that if an edible plant looks well-tended or maintained by someone (netted, pruned etc.), it's bad form to 'obtain a yield' from it unless it's got a sign saying 'help yourself'.

If you see a plant dripping with edible parts in someone's garden, try knocking on the door and asking whether you can pick a bit. You may get a 'no', but I've found it's more often a 'yes', and I've built some great Community by meeting other food-growers this way. If you see an introduced fruit tree planted in public and the ground is littered with fallen, decaying fruit, that's usually a fair indicator that you won't upset anyone by harvesting a bit.

A caution when foraging fruit

No matter where you're foraging, it's important not to spread pests and disease. Around the world, various species of fruit fly have the potential to decimate fruit-growing regions, and in most areas, there are viruses, borers, moths and weevils that can have equally devastating effects on food production. You can do your bit by knowing what to look for in affected plant matter, and ensuring you don't transport fruit afflicted by pests and disease to new areas.

Some basic rules and etiquette

I found it much easier to be an ethical forager once I'd devised a few simple rules to follow. Here's my go-to thinking:

1   Commit to the long game. Spend time (at least a year) observing any new foraging location to make sure it's appropriate and safe to forage there.

2   Never pick and use any plant you wouldn't feel confident feeding to your best friend's child. Hyper-vigilance is advised, as there's no one 'checking your homework', and the risks of harm are real if you get it wrong.

3   Don't damage the plant or the surrounding environment.

4   Follow the 'rule of quarters' (see right).

5   There'll be other opportunities. If you don't obtain a yield today, it's part of the bigger picture.

'Rule of quarters'

You can't assume that all of a plant will reach maturity after you've departed, so it's important to apply self-regulation when considering which parts are available for harvesting. Take stock of what's mature and ready to be harvested right then and there, then apply the rule of quarters.

Of the food that is ripe and ready to pick when you are there, leave at least:

+   a quarter for the animals, birds and insects who rely on it for food

+   a quarter for the health and success of the plant itself

+   a quarter for other foragers who may come along.

Of the remaining quarter, actively consider:

+   what you truly need

+   what you will use in the next two to three days

+   how you will prepare or preserve it.

Let the answers to these questions guide how much of the remaining quarter you harvest.

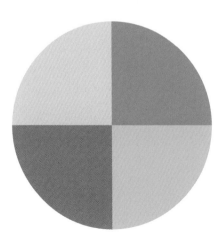

Getting started

If ethical foraging sounds like it's for you, it's time to get into the details of how to do it. First learn how to keep yourself physically safe out in the field; then it's all about plant specifics.

Risky business?

Is it really that risky to forage for food? Well, yes and no. There are certainly more risks foraging for food than shopping at the local greengrocer, but don't let that deter you. Risks have to be mentioned for safety's sake, else I'd be a terrible teacher, but I promise that the fun and satisfaction of foraging safely far outweighs any risks! I want to help you feel empowered, knowledgeable and keen to get out there. And the truth is, if you pack your Sensible Hat in your foraging kit, you'll stay safe and happy, and build up your knowledge quickly. So with that in mind, let's cover off the serious business first.

There's a saying among foragers that's designed to make new learners stop and think. It goes 'Technically, everything's edible. Sometimes only once though', meaning there's nothing stopping you from eating any foraged specimen you like, but if you get your ID wrong, it may just be the last thing you ever eat. Morbid, yes; but it's been proven true a few too many times, so it's worth bringing up.

There's another saying that's a bit more helpful, and designed to keep you safe: 'If in doubt, leave it out.' Essentially, it means if there's any doubt about whether you've got a plant ID 100% right, or you can't tell if it's been affected by contaminants, then you should simply leave it out of your basket. Far better to be safe than sorry. If you want to grow into an *old* forager, a slice of proverbial humble pie can keep you happy and safe when you're first learning to identify edible plants. Don't be embarrassed when you get an ID wrong to begin with: I say 'when' not 'if' because it happens to us all!

Enjoy the journey
Rob Gould, @cotswoldforager, United Kingdom

'There are many easy wins in foraging, especially for beginners, [so don't be] put off by potential issues that you won't encounter until much later on your journey.'

Death, dinner and druids
Tom Radford, eatthecountry.com, United Kingdom

'I think people should forage to connect to their past and understand that this wasn't a hobby, it was survival. Learn the stories, the folklore and the anecdotes. And just have fun!'

Knowledge is power

Building plant knowledge takes time. It is estimated there are close to half a million plant species on Earth, and while there are lots of edible ones, there are just as many inedible ones. To confidently ID an edible plant, it's really important to know whether it has any lookalikes. There are quite a lot of notable look-alike plants out there, and there are some you really don't want to mix up (like wild carrot and poison hemlock, for example). So the first question to ask when you *think* you know what a plant is, is 'What *isn't* it?'. This will guide you to look for nasty doppelgängers, thus keeping you safe.

1   Poison hemlock – does what it says on the box (i.e. toxic)

2   Elderflower – some parts edible

3   Wild carrot – some parts edible

Another thing to be aware of as you learn about wild foods is that some plants have parts that are edible as well as parts that are toxic to humans. Any foraging guidebook worth its salt will make sure you're aware of this, so don't be too frightened. Simply be aware that just because something has a tasty fruit that you've seen in processed products at the supermarket doesn't mean you can chow down on a handful of them in the wild.

An example of this is elderberry: elderberry flowers are used to make cordial and cocktails, and their berries are used in lots of herbal supplements. But everything aside from the flowers and the flesh of the *ripe* berries is really quite toxic, including the stems and seeds. You should remove as much stem material as possible and strain out any seeds when using elderberry, and you should definitely avoid ingesting any leaves, bark or roots from the plant.

Similarly, some plants are innocent enough on their own, but can interact with existing medical conditions or medications. For example, you should limit your consumption of *Oxalis* species if you're prone to kidney stones, and common hawthorn can interact with blood pressure medication unless it's cooked a certain way. Again though, good foraging guides will warn you of these things.

Now, before you run away, never to pick another plant for fear of poisoning yourself, please know that I carefully selected the plants in this foraging guide to be encouraging and confidence-building for new foragers. The plants can be found in most countries in the world, and if you check off the ID points in the guide, you'd have to be trying *very* hard to get it wrong. I've also chosen plants on the basis that if they *do* happen to have a lookalike, it's not a nasty one. Feeling better? Excellent, let's push on.

Introduce wild foods to your diet slowly

Wild foods haven't been cultivated for their digestibility like the commercially grown plants we're used to. Always introduce new foraged foods to your diet in small doses, so you can make sure that a) you're not allergic to them, and b) your body has a chance to get used to processing them.

Physical safety

Often, wild and feral food plants are found along edges and margins such as roadsides, ditches and railway lines. In many countries, it's illegal to get close to railway tracks, so they're usually off the cards as a foraging location, no matter how much tasty fennel grows there. It can also be challenging to reach plants growing along these types of edges, so before you enter an area to forage, always assess not only the legality of entering that area, but also your physical capacity to do so safely. Also consider environmental dangers that could turn a foraging jaunt into a hospital visit: sunstroke, dehydration, snakes, spiders, leeches, ticks. These risks will vary depending on your location.

You can prepare by doing simple things like knowing where particular creepy-crawlies like to hang out, and how to avoid them; scanning and testing any unfamiliar ground for hazardous patches, and wearing bright clothing so passing traffic can see you. Wearing protective clothing and carrying a first-aid kit, water and a phone are also good moves.

Contaminants

There are quite a few contaminants that could make even a correctly identified plant unsafe to eat. Consider whether the following could have affected the plant you're hoping to forage, and avoid areas you think could be contaminated by them:

+ **Road run-off**

+ **Fumes from traffic or factories**

+ **Chemicals from factories**

+ **Soil contamination (lead, radiation)**

+ **Animal waste and parasites in the waste**

+ **Human waste.**

It's often not possible to know whether contaminants have affected an area, and that's another good reason to observe a location for a while before picking anything. You'll notice plants start to suffer within weeks if they've been exposed to something really nasty.

Learn to ID plants

Still with me? It might feel as though a lot of what I've covered so far is reason enough never to go foraging, but truly, I've gone into detail because I think you'll feel much safer if you have a proper idea of what you need to worry about. I figure that if you've been told what's *actually* worth worrying about, that frees up the rest of your thinking space for useful, accurate learning.

The very best way to learn about plant identification is to head out with a seasoned, reputable expert. What you can learn in person – where you're able to see, feel, scratch, sniff and even taste examples safely – surpasses anything you could ever learn from books and online resources.

The second best way to learn is to sharpen your observation skills, read *all* the books, and practise a lot so you can develop your own personal style of knowledge. Many foraging guidebooks use technical or scientific language to describe plant parts, as this is the most effective way to relay precise information. Rather than being daunted by this, I like to come up with my own quirky ways to remember ID features of plants that are in line with the technical-speak.

For example, 'umbel' is the name given to flowers that grow in an umbrella shape (the words have the same origin), so whenever I see the word 'umbel' in a field guide, I picture a plant filled with little pixies and gnomes using the flowers to keep the rain off. It's silly, but it works, and I feel more confident using technical guides as a result.

Begin paying attention to plants around you: you could start keeping a journal to record observations of particular plants. Take photos, use a magnifying glass, take samples home to observe over time. Start noticing the size, shape and texture of plant parts; notice how plants grow (e.g. as vines vs with branches); pay attention to smells and colours; count how many leaves or petals a plant part has. Notice every part of plants: leaves, stems, flowers, fruits, seeds, roots, and even growth patterns, like the whorls of pine cones.

If you can hone these observation skills through practice, in conjunction with researching with trusted guides and learning materials, you'll increase your capacity as a forager steadily over time.

Plant ID apps

Lots of people use smartphone apps to identify plant species. While they're a great place to start hunting for an ID, they're a terrible place to stop. They can be helpful in directing your further research, but I'd never rely on an app for a positive plant ID. I urge extreme caution in using them to identify something you wish to eat.

Useful equipment

Other than reputable learning materials, you don't technically *need* anything to go foraging, but there are a few things that make it easier. Sturdy waterproof boots are a good investment: they'll keep you warm and dry in winter, and can help protect you from snakes and brambles in summer. A folding knife can be really useful, and in my opinion you can never have too many baskets or bags, especially around summer and autumn when it's peak foraging season. Op shops and tip shops are great for getting these on the cheap. Here's a checklist of handy stuff.

Foraging kit

+ Foraging and identification guidebooks

+ Sturdy shoes or boots (waterproof)

+ Long pants and sleeves (for snake, sun and spike protection)

+ Sun hat

+ Sunscreen

+ Baskets or foraging pouches

+ Folding knife

+ Forked walking stick

+ Hiking first-aid kit, including a snake-bite kit

+ Lightweight water bottle

+ Phone.

Places to look

Given that plants have developed mechanisms to use animals as part of their seed-dispersal strategy, it's no wonder that many of the plants we call 'weeds' are actually spread by humans. This is true of cultivated plants too: scattered around regions where humans have settled over the decades, you will often find wild versions of the plants we recognise from the greengrocer or supermarket – think of the thistly looking weedy artichokes known as cardoons that grow along country roadways, for example.

As a forager in Australia, I like to view maps through a historical lens, because I know I'm more likely to find edible invasive species of plants where European settlers set up shop. So I'll spend time exploring regions that had bustling townships during the Gold Rush era, or look to areas where native vegetation was cleared so European homesteads could be established. 'Traditional' edible plants like fruit trees and shrubby berries were often imported for planting around these homesteads, and their descendants can still be found around these locations. Farmlands where birds, small animals and reptiles flock to the fences provide margins where brambles, weedy and seedy greens, and small fruits like elderberry and hawthorn love to grow.

Having said all of this, I say your immediate neighbourhood is the best classroom when you're looking to develop your plant observation skills. If you have a yard where you can allow a patch of grass to grow untended, it's almost certain that within a month you'll have edible weeds popping up. Then you can practise your ID skills regularly with ease, and feel safe tasting those weeds (or not) with an intimate knowledge of what (if any) contaminants they've come into contact with.

What to look for when

Once you've begun observing the nature around you, you'll notice all sorts of things about how and when plants go through developmental changes. Most plants go through the following cycles: sprout, flower, fruit, seed dispersal.

Sure, some plants reproduce differently, but when you understand that the basic pattern all living things follow is 'survive, thrive, reproduce', it becomes easier to know when different parts of plants will be reaching the stage where you want to harvest them. For example, if you want to collect wild fennel seeds to use in tea or as a spice, then noticing when local fennel plants are in bloom, producing prominent yellow umbels (flower clusters shaped like umbrellas), will give you a heads-up that seed-harvesting time is on the horizon.

Here are a few common plants to look out for in your area each season:

SPRING

+ Dandelion (flowers and roots)
+ Elderflowers
+ Fat hen
+ Magnolias
+ Pine tree parts, edible (pollen and cones)
+ Prickly pear paddles (leaves)
+ Purslane
+ Rock samphire
+ Roses, wild
+ Three-cornered leek
+ Violets, English
+ Weedy greens

SUMMER

+ Apples
+ Blackberries
+ Dandelion flowers
+ Elderberries
+ Fennel, wild (pollen and greens)
+ Figs
+ Green walnuts
+ Mulberries
+ Plums, wild
+ Prickly pear fruit
+ Purslane
+ Rosehips
+ Stone fruits (peaches, nectarines etc.)

AUTUMN

+ Apples
+ Brassicas, wild
+ Chestnuts
+ Damson plums
+ Elderberries
+ Fennel seeds
+ Hawthorn
+ Mallow root
+ Pears
+ Quince
+ Rosehip
+ Sloes
+ Walnuts

WINTER

+ Bittercress
+ Brassicas, wild
+ Chickweed
+ Dandelion (roots and leaves)
+ Hawthorn
+ Medlars
+ Oxalis
+ Pine tree parts, edible (needles, cones and pollen)
+ Radish, wild
+ Three-cornered leek
+ Violets, wild
+ Weedy greens

'Foraging allows me to live more seasonally and become familiar with the growing patterns of plants. I believe that eating what's in season is great for me, but it also feels essential to know what grows when, where I live. We're so removed from our own food-growing knowledge. Living in an inner-city sharehouse with a small yard, we don't have space to grow much – foraging lets me connect with the seasons. It's a relationship, between forager and nature, and it allows us to develop care about the health of the trees, the soil, the plants, fellow animals and foragers. It's a really fun and rewarding activity, and I'd love for more yet-to-be foragers to know it!'

What to make with your finds

There is so much you can do with foraged fruit that it's worth keeping a list of recipes to make when opportunity and seasonal abundance knocks. Whatever you choose, be sure it's something you can manage to get done within a few days so the food you foraged doesn't spoil.

+ Jam, jelly, paste

+ Chutney, sauce

+ Cordial

+ Bottled or canned fruit

+ Stewed and frozen fruit

+ Dried fruit – pieces or fruit leather

+ Pickles or ferments

+ Fermented wine or soda

+ Infused vinegar

+ Infused spirits.

Now that you're loaded up with considerations to take into account when foraging, it's time to learn about eight tasty wild edibles and what you can make with them.

Apples

Malus spp.

Growing with very little love, producing mammoth yields when happy, and giving us easily recognisable fruit that can be stored for months and months, the feral apple tree is a forager's dream.

Most modern domesticated apples (*Malus domestica*) evolved from hybrids of an ancient wild apple in Kazakhstan (*Malus sieversii*) and European crabapples (*Malus sylvestris*). Feral apples often grow from seed dispersed by animals or humans, and these days that seed is usually the result of cross-pollination between unknown parent trees, varieties of either *M. domestica* or *M. sylvestris*, or both. As a result, the fruit varies dramatically from one feral tree to the next. You'll likely find that feral apples taste less sweet than you're accustomed to, but knowing how useful and versatile they are makes them welcome fruit regardless.

Cultivated species (numbering around 7,500) tend to be grafted onto strong-growing apple or crabapple rootstock, whereas feral apple trees often exhibit a trade-off between growth habit and fruit size. That is, they may grow massive but have small, average fruit, or they may have delicious fruit but be scrawny, scraggly trees.

A good feral apple harvest can be used in baking, cooking, preserving, drink- and sweet-making, dehydrating, and even making low-tox cleaning solutions: definitely worth the effort of learning how to identify them!

ID POINTS

Branches and shape (1)
Apples are very 'tree-shaped' trees, with a short, stout trunk and many gnarled branches forming a rounded canopy up to 10 m/32 feet tall. The skin is silvery-greyish brown, with older branches often sporting lichen the colour of sulphur or sea mist. Short fruiting spurs (which look as though they're wearing stockings that are falling down) are found along longer branches. Being deciduous, apple trees lose their leaves in autumn, leaving bare branches until spring.

Leaves (2)
The leaves are 5–10 cm/2–4 inches long, ovate (oval, or as I like to say, 'leaf-shaped'), mid-green leaves with slightly serrated edges. The sturdy stem transitions to a central vein with alternating offshoot veins. The underside is paler than the top and may sport a silverish-white fuzz.

Flowers (3)
An apple tree in full blossom is quite a spectacle. The froth of flowers emerge from silverish-white fuzzy buds in groups of five or six on short fruiting spurs growing along longer branches. Each flower, 3–5 cm/1¼–2 inches wide, has five rounded petals that are typically white with a pink blush. The central pistil with up to five sticky stigmas captures pollen from the numerous stamens when it is spread by pollinating insects.

Fruit (4)
You'd be hard-pressed to find someone who doesn't know what apples look like, but feral apples often vary significantly from what we see at supermarkets. They are fleshy fruits, round to slightly ovate in shape. Typically the flesh is white to cream, firm, crunchy and juicy. The skin can be green, yellow, pink, red or a combination of these, often with flecks or striations in darker colours. Five central carpels (like wombs) hold up to five seeds each and resemble a star when the fruit is cut across the middle.

Toxic look-alikes
Apples are related to many other edible fruits, as they are part of the larger Rosaceae family (which includes rosehips, pears, quince, crabapples, medlars and nashis, to name a few). All apples bear technically edible fruit, but if you've ever bitten into a small crabby apple and instantly felt your face implode from the sourness, you'll know that some are definitely more palatable than others!

Where and when to find them

Because apples are such a common snack food, feral trees are often found along roadsides or walking tracks in temperate to cold climates, where cores have been discarded by humans or animals. Hedgerows and abandoned settlements around the world are often dotted with older trees planted by Eurocentric settlers. As apples are a favourite treat for horses, it's also quite common to find apple trees surrounding equine paddocks.

Look for apple trees all year round: their distinctive growth habit and bark colour make them easy to spot even when bare. Leaves emerge and flowers bloom from early spring to mid-summer, and the petals fall shortly after pollination. Look for ripe apples from late summer to late autumn.

How to use them

Flowers: tea, confections, syrup, garnishes

Fruit: jam, jelly, paste, leather, vinegar, baking, desserts, fresh eating, salads, roasted, dried, mulled wine, tea, pectin stock

Wood: carving, smoking food

She'll be apples

Apples keep for a really long time. Store them in a single layer somewhere cool and check them once a month to remove any damaged fruit. They will wrinkle and sweeten with time, which makes them ideal for baking and brewing tea with.

Festive spiced apple jelly

Makes 8–10 jars, 270 ml/9 fl oz each

Wild apples typically have high pectin levels, which means they're ideal for making preserved jelly with because the pectin helps achieve a firm 'set'. This jelly takes around a day to produce because you need to let time do some work for you, so it's a good one to start in the evening and complete the next day.

The glowing, clear ruby-red result is a perfect way to instantly upgrade a cheese platter. It's just as at home in baked goods, as an accompaniment to roast dinners, in marinades, or simply slathered on toast.

INGREDIENTS

2 kg/4 lb 6 oz tart apples,* washed

1 cinnamon quill

10 allspice (pimento) berries

5 green cardamom pods

5 cloves

1 star anise

2–3 kg (10–15 cups) sugar

Juice of 3–5 lemons

NOTE

*If you have access to quinces, medlars, crabapples or hawthorn, you can use any of these as the base for this preserve.

**You can deal with the leftover fruit pulp by using it in baking (push it through a sieve or mouli first to remove the cores and spices) or composting it.

METHOD

1   Chop the apples roughly, including the skins and cores. Add them to a large pot.

2   Add the spices and barely cover everything with water.

3   Simmer over medium heat until the fruit is very soft. Top up the water if it drops below fruit level.

4   Scald a clean tea towel (dish towel) or muslin cloth in boiling water, then use it to line a colander placed over a large bowl.

5   Carefully pour the contents of the pot into the lined colander. Tie the corners of the cloth together to form a bag.

6   Hang the bag from a sturdy spot above the bowl. Leave it for three to six hours (or overnight) for all the liquid to drip into the bowl. *Do not* squeeze the bag, or you will end up with cloudy jelly.**

7   Measure the strained liquid into a large, heavy-based pot.

8   For every 4 cups of liquid, add 3 cups of sugar and the juice of one lemon.

9   Stir over medium heat until the sugar is dissolved, then bring to the boil.

10 Keep the liquid at a rolling boil until it reaches setting point. To test for a set, drip a little hot liquid onto a cold plate. Allow to cool, then run your finger through it: it will wrinkle if it's reached setting point.

11 Remove from the heat, skim any scum from the top, then pour the jelly into hot sterilised jars and seal them tight with sterilised lids while still hot.

12 Store in a cool, dark cupboard, then in the fridge once opened.

Blackberries

Rubus fruticosus

Blackberry is one of the easiest forageable plants to identify, and it has potential to fruit heavily, making it a desirable find for foragers. Found in rural and suburban areas alike, it spreads via seeds, cutting, roots and layered propagation (long canes touch the ground away from the middle of a patch and grow roots there to form a 'daughter plant'). As a result, it is a declared noxious weed in every state and territory of Australia except the Northern Territory, and foragers must ensure they do not contribute to its spread.

Because of this, it's common for blackberries to be sprayed with herbicide during spring and autumn in public places. This poses a problem for foragers, as it often isn't possible to determine whether plants in the wild have been treated with chemicals that could be harmful if ingested. Affected plants will begin to show signs of distress in the form of yellowed, curled leaves, sometimes growing abnormally, a while after spraying, which is why it's particularly important to observe blackberry plants long-term (for 12 months or more) before electing to pick the fruit.

Once you know you've found an unsprayed place to forage blackberries from, be sure to wear appropriate protective clothing while picking. A thick long-sleeved top, long thick pants (jeans are ideal) and closed footwear are advised. Use a sturdy forked stick or even a fence paling to push down long prickly canes; it allows you to move further into the patch and reach the juiciest, plumpest berries, which are *always* in the middle.

If you do happen to get snagged by one of the many thorns, rather than pull away, take hold of the offending cane between the prickles and lean in: this generally releases you from the backward-curving thorns.

Blackberry brambles provide food and protective shelter for small birds and rodents, so be aware that snakes (if they're present in the region) may also share the space. Moving slowly, thumping the ground with your feet or a stick and making noise as you move towards a bramble patch are good ways to warn them off before you pick. And because all of these animals can spread disease and parasites, wash any scratches you sustain from thorns, and wash all fruit very well before eating it.

ID POINTS

Leaves and stems (1+2)

Long arching canes (3–6 m/10–20 feet) with many leaves grow in the first year, beginning bright green and ageing to dark green–purple. Second-year growth consists of multiple offshoots along first-year canes, each growing leaves and sprays of flowers (racemes). All stems feature sharp, backward-arching thorns.

Leaves are compound, with three to five ovate leaflets, mid-green on top with slight silverish fuzz underneath. Margins are lightly serrated, and the undersides of mid-veins feature sharp thorns.

Flowers (3)

Flowers grow in racemes at the end of second-year shoots. Each flower measures 3–5 cm/1¼–2 inches across and has five white and pink rounded petals surrounding many stamens and a central pale green carpel fringed with numerous stigmas.

Fruits (4)

Each fruit is an aggregate of small, round fleshy segments (called drupelets), each housing a seed. Fruits begin small, green and hard, growing larger and softer and turning first red then black as they ripen. When they are glossy black–purple and come off the stalk easily, they are ripe.

> #### Toxic look-alikes
> There are other bramble berries in the *Rubus* genus that look similar to blackberry, but none bear toxic fruit.

Where and when to find them

Blackberries grow on every continent except Antarctica, and they are extremely adaptable, so they can be found in a wide variety of climates in cool, temperate and arid regions. They prefer moist, well-drained soil with moderate to full sun.

Blackberries are spread by birds and rodents, and the seeds often fall along fence lines in rural areas: paddocks, hedgerows etc. They can also be found along creek beds and gullies, but without adequate sunshine, they will not fruit heavily there.

Look for flowers in mid- to late spring, and berries from mid-summer through to autumn.

How to use them

Leaves: Pick the tender young leaves in spring, ferment them in 2% brine, then dehydrate and use as a caffeine-free alternative to green tea. (For details of the method, see the recipe for dried fermented three-cornered leek on page 201.) Note: blackberry leaf tea is listed as 'use with caution in pregnancy', as insufficient studies have been done to ensure its safety for babies in utero. Avoid the leaves if you are pregnant.

Fruit: jam, jelly, fruit paste, cordial, liqueur, fruit wine, fruit leather, wild soda, kombucha, fruit vinegar, smoothies, baking and more

Boozy blackberry and apple jam

Makes 8–10 jars, 270 ml/9 fl oz each

Late summer is the time for bramble berries and apples, and this sumptuous jam is an annual favourite at my place.

It calls for a hefty slurp of sloe gin, but if you've had a go at making your own infused booze with wild fruit – something like plum pudding brandy (see page 186) – by all means use that instead. Alternatively, use any clean-tasting spirit, or simply leave out the alcohol altogether.

INGREDIENTS

1 kg/2 lb 3 oz blackberries, washed, stalks removed

1.5 kg/3 lb 5 oz sugar

1 kg/2 lb 3 oz tart apples, peeled, cored and chopped

1 lemon, washed and halved

½ cup sloe gin

METHOD

1   Mix the blackberries and about two-thirds of the sugar (1 kg/1 lb 7 oz) in a bowl. Set aside to macerate* for two to three hours.

2   Combine the apples and 2 cups water in a wide, heavy-based pot. Bring to the boil over high heat, then reduce heat to medium and simmer until the apples are mushy.

3   Add the blackberries and remaining sugar, then squeeze in the lemon juice and add the lemon halves as well.

4   Bring to the boil over medium–high heat, stirring gently to dissolve the sugar.

5   Continue cooking at a rolling boil until the jam reaches setting point. To test for a set, drip a little hot jam onto a cold plate. Allow to cool, then run your finger through it: it will wrinkle if it's reached setting point.

6   Remove from the heat, skim any scum from the top, fish out the lemon halves, then stir in the sloe gin. Let the jam sit for five minutes off the heat, then stir. This helps to distribute the berries evenly.

7   Pour the jam into hot sterilised jars and seal them tight with sterilised lids while hot.

8   Store in a cool, dark cupboard, then in the fridge once opened.

NOTE

*Macerating soft fruit means letting the sugar draw liquid from the fruit. The liquid dissolves the sugar, which allows the fruit to cook more quickly when you put it on the heat, and this means the jam turns out looking brighter and tasting fresher.

Chickweed

Stellaria media

'If it's got bones like a chicken, and a comb like a chicken, it's chickweed!'

This saying has been around for donkey's yonks, and it's a nifty one to remember when you're searching for this easy-growing leafy green weed, because it describes two of the plant's defining features: the strong central veins throughout the stems (bones), and the mohawk of hairs along one side of the stems (like a chicken's comb).

Found easily in gardens and parks, chickweed is a great edible weed to kickstart your foraging lessons because it has several identifying features that you'd have to try pretty hard to muck up. Also, it has flavour and nutrient values similar to those of soft butter lettuce, making it easy to add to your diet.

ID POINTS

Leaves and stems (1+2)

Leaves are pale grass-green, ovate with a pointed tip, in opposite pairs with distance between each pair along multiple stems growing from a central base. Branching stems grow up to 40 cm/16 inches long and have distinct identifying features of a strong clear central vein with clear sap, and a single line of curved hairs (like a mohawk!) that grows along the stem on alternating sides, switching sides between each pair of leaves. Roots are shallow, white and hair-like, growing from the centre of a sprawling rosette of stems.

Flowers (3)

Teeny-tiny (less than 1 cm/⅜ inch across), self-fertile, unscented flowers grow from the stems on delicate short stalks. Surrounded by five-pointed hairy green sepals, the five white petals are so deeply lobed that they look like 10 petals. The central pale-yellow stigma with three sticky styles are surrounded by three to eight reddish-violet stamens.

Fruits

Small seed pods bear many dark brown, yellowish or reddish-brown seeds, nearly circular and up to 1 mm/³⁄₆₄ inch across.

Where and when to find it

Chickweed favours cool, damp but well-drained soil, and a bit of sun, hence it tends to be found during the temperate/cooler months of the year. Being a tender plant, it doesn't do well in frost or too much heat, which will affect which months you'll find it around the world. As a general rule, when you start seeing lots of fungi action in parks and gardens, it's highly possible you'll find chickweed nearby.

Keep an eye out in pots and garden beds, as chickweed loves slightly disturbed soil. It can also be found in great carpets under shady trees in many grassed parklands.

How to use it

Leaves: salads, Catie pie (see page 165), pesto, soups, sandwiches, pakoras, smoothies

Chickweed can also be used medicinally as a skin salve or poultice to reduce inflammation and itching.

Toxic look-alikes

Scarlet pimpernel (*Anagallis arvensis*) (5) and **petty spurge** (*Euphorbia peplus*) (6) both loosely resemble chickweed, but close observation of their flowers and stem shape will quickly help you to see the difference.

Various sub-species of chickweed are found around the world, so if you find a look-alike, it's worth investigating further because you may have come across another edible weed.

1 + 3

2

2

5 Toxic look-alike

6 Toxic look-alike

Catie pie (weedy greens pie)

Serves 2

Winter heralds the arrival of an abundance of leafy green veggies and weeds that are delicious and full of nutrients. Things like chickweed, dandelion, sow thistle, bittercress and wild brassica work well in loads of winter meals, but Catie pie (named after the dear friend who first introduced me to this clever way of cooking weeds) is definitely a favourite.

Because it uses whatever you have on any given day, the pie will never be exactly the same as the last one you made, but this recipe is a good starting point. Adjust it to suit your circumstances and preferences.

For extra protein and crunch, include some chopped toasted nuts or seeds – chestnuts, almonds, walnuts, pine nuts and sunflower seeds all work well.

INGREDIENTS

6–7 cups fresh greens*

3–4 mushrooms (cultivated or wild)

3–4 garlic cloves

Olive oil, for frying

2 eggs (or equivalent in egg replacement)

¼ cup cheese (mozzarella, feta, goat's cheese, blue, brie, camembert: dealer's choice), coarsely grated or chopped

1 sheet puff pastry

Milk, water or extra egg, beaten, for glazing

NOTE

*Chickweed, bittercress, dandelion, sow thistle, mizuna, nasturtium, kale, brassicas of all sorts, spring onions, sorrel, rainbow chard, spinach, broccoli stems, cauliflower leaves, onions, dill, zucchini, Asian greens … they all work well.

METHOD

1   Preheat the oven to 180°C/350°F.

2   Wash the greens and mushrooms well.

3   Finely chop the garlic, greens and mushrooms.

4   Fry the garlic in a good splash of olive oil over medium heat until golden.

5   Add the tougher veg (brassicas, silverbeet stems, chard stems) to the pan. Stir until wilted.

6   Add the mushrooms and fry for a few minutes.

7   Add the tender greens (mizuna, herbs, weeds). Stir until wilted.

8   Turn off the heat and allow everything to cool slightly.

9   Crack the eggs into the pan and mix well. Season to taste with salt and pepper.

10   Transfer the mix to a pie dish and stir in the cheese.

11   Cover with puff pastry, cut a steam vent in the centre and brush with milk, water or egg.

12   Bake until golden brown (20–25 minutes).

Weedy greens pesto

Makes about 4 cups

Late winter and spring brings an abundance of fresh weedy greens and herbs to many gardens. Rather than contaminating your patch with chemical sprays to get rid of them, why not eat the problem? You can 'obtain a yield' by 'catching and storing' the nutritional energy in weeds with this simple recipe.

Greens to consider adding include dandelion, three-cornered leek, chickweed, parsley, bittercress, nasturtium, celery leaves and even carrot tops. Pesto is a brilliant thing to make when you're doing a seasonal changeover in the garden (pulling out old crops and planting new ones), as you can use just about any edible raw greens to bulk it out.

Use it as a dip, sandwich spread or pasta sauce, add it to potato or pasta salad, or have a go at making pinwheels using puff pastry schmeared with pesto and dotted with feta. Or freeze it in ice-cube trays to use as a nutrient and flavour booster throughout the year.

INGREDIENTS

1 large handful unsalted roasted nuts (your choice)

2 large garlic cloves, peeled

1 tsp salt

6–8 cups fresh edible weeds and soft herbs

1–1½ cups olive oil

Juice of 1 small lemon

100 g/3½ oz grated parmesan or nutritional yeast

METHOD

1   Wash and thoroughly dry the weeds and herbs. Remove tough stalks and older leaves (they're likely bitter).

2   Blitz the nuts, garlic and salt in a food processor until roughly chopped.

3   Fill the food processor with greens and a good big drizzle of oil. Blitz until reduced in volume by half.

4   Add more greens and oil and blitz again until smooth, adding more oil as needed to achieve a smooth consistency.

5   Repeat until all the greens have been incorporated.

6   Add the lemon juice and grated parmesan or nutritional yeast. Blitz to combine.

7   Spoon into jars and top with olive oil. Pesto will keep in the fridge for 5–7 days or in the freezer for up to 6 months.

Dandelion

Taraxacum officinale

Dandelion is one of the easiest plants to start your foraging journey with. All parts of the plant are edible – leaves, roots, flower buds, flowers, even the seeds. It has plenty of easy defining features to help you tell it apart from its many close relatives, but most of its look-alikes are edible too, so the chances of getting into trouble are low.

Native to Eurasia, dandelion has been naturalised in many of the world's temperate zones. Technically there are around 2500 species, but the variation between these is so slight that they have all been lumped under the name *Taraxacum officinale*.

The English name 'dandelion' comes from the French *dent-de-lion*, meaning tooth of the lion, referring to the jagged-toothed appearance of the leaves. I'm a big one for using visual mnemonics to help me remember plant species, and the image of a lion works well for me when I'm trying to tell it apart from its close cousins: large flower, ruffled 'mane', large sharp 'teeth' along the leaves, and easy to spot in a field.

Whether you're picking the leaves to use in a salad, weed pie or pesto, gathering the flowers to brew up into floral champagne or to make into a vegan alternative to honey, digging the roots to make a coffee substitute, or picking the flower buds to make pickled 'poor man's capers', there's something for everyone in dandelion. And given how loaded it is with vitamins and nutrients, chances are you'll never see this plant as an unwanted weed again!

ID POINTS

Leaves and stems (1 + 2)
Light to mid-green, 5–50 cm (2–20 inches) long and 1–10 cm (½–4 inches) wide, the leaves emerge from the central taproot to form a rosette. The rosette grows flat to the ground if the plant is solitary and

exposed, and more upright in shaded, crowded positions. The leaves are thin and tender (like those of butter lettuce), and their surface is smooth or features a few weak hairs. They are lanceolate (long and pointed at the tip), with edges that are lobed to resemble sharp 'teeth'. The depth of the lobes depends on the growing situation: they can be very pronounced or so slight that the leaf appears almost ovate (see the photo on page 169). The leaf colour often changes to purple then white towards the base.

The long cream-white taproot, 15 cm–1 m (6 inches–3 feet 3 inches) long and 2–5 cm (¾–2 inches) wide, exudes bitter white latex when damaged. Some smaller, thinner roots emerge from the taproot. The plant will regrow several rosettes of leaves if broken off at ground level. *Avoid overconsumption, as dandelion root is a diuretic and laxative.*

Flowers (3)
Large yellow flower heads 4–5 cm/1½–2 inches wide emerge from tight green buds comprising an outer set of sepals that freely curve down towards the stem (like a ruffled Shakespearean collar) and an inner set that protect the flower between growing phases. The inner set of sepals opens to reveal what look like flower petals, but which are actually hundreds of tiny ray florets, each capable of producing one seed.

Multiple flowers may grow from one plant, one flower head per stalk. The stalks, which are hollow, range from 5 cm to 80 cm (2 inches to 2 feet 7 inches) long, are light green changing to purple then white towards the base, and exude bitter white latex when broken.

Fruits (4)
Once a dandelion flower head has been pollinated, the inner set of sepals closes around spent florets while seeds form. After roughly 10 days, the sepals open to allow many seeds – each sporting a white, hairy 'parachute' (called a pappus) around 6 mm/¼ inch wide – to expand into a globe structure known commonly as a 'clock'.

5

Toxic look-alikes

There are plenty of cousins in the broader dandelion family that bear some resemblance to it, including **cat's ear** (*Hypochaeris radicata*) (5), **sow thistle** (*Sonchus oleraceus*) (6), hawkbit (*Leontodon* spp.) and even chicory (*Cichorium intybus*), but they are all edible.

Aside from these, the only other vaguely look-alike plant to avoid confusing with dandelion is **wild lettuce** (*Lactuca virosa*) (7). It is edible, but it has a soporific effect (it makes you sleepy). Wild lettuce should be eaten with knowledge and care as just one or two leaves could make you very drowsy and could interact with other medications.

6

Where and when to find it

Dandelion can be found year-round in truly temperate zones; elsewhere, it grows mainly from spring to autumn. It prefers damp, slightly shaded soil, but it can be found growing almost anywhere – on farmland, in gardens, among undisturbed native vegetation, along margins of industrial areas, even between bricks and concrete pavers.

Harvest the flower buds (to make pickled caper alternatives) during late spring, the flowers throughout summer, and the taproots (to make a coffee alternative) at the end of winter. Leaves can be harvested any time, but like all weeds, they taste least bitter when picked young.

7 **Use with caution**

How to use it

Roots: roast for tea, coffee

Leaves: salads, pies, spanakopita, pesto, smoothies, soups, stock

Flowers: champagne, fritters, soda, vegan 'honey', tea, garnish, pickled 'capers' (unopened buds)

Dandelion-spiced chai latte

Makes 1 pot of chai

Dandelion root has been used for many years as a coffee substitute, particularly in times of coffee scarcity. Being in the same family as chicory, it has bitter, rich and nutty flavours that make it an excellent base for hot drink infusions, especially if you're after a caffeine-free beverage.

It takes a *lot* of roasted dandelion roots to make a single pot of dandelion 'coffee', and these days it's hard to find large fields of weeds that haven't been sprayed with contaminants. This warm-spiced chai is a great alternative if you're able to forage only smaller amounts of dandelion root.

INGREDIENTS

2 tbsp ground roasted dandelion root*

5 cm/2 inch piece of ginger, unpeeled, chopped

1 cinnamon stick, crushed

5 cloves

3 green cardamom pods

1 tsp wild fennel seed

4 cups of water

¼ cup sugar (white, brown or otherwise – dealer's choice)

2 cups dairy milk or plant milk of your choice

METHOD

1   Combine the dandelion root, ginger and spices in a saucepan. Cover with the water and bring to the boil over medium–high heat.

2   Reduce the heat to low–medium and simmer for 10–15 minutes, until the chai is dark and aromatic.

3   Add the milk and sugar. Stir to dissolve the sugar, then simmer for 10–15 minutes, until you're happy with the taste.

4   Strain through a tea strainer and serve hot.

How to roast and grind dandelion roots

1   Wash the roots well.

2   Chop them into smaller pieces and dry thoroughly in a dehydrator, an oven or the sun.

3   Roast the pieces in an oven at 180°C/350°F for 10 minutes, then crush into smaller pieces.

4   Roast for another 10 minutes, then blitz in a food processor until finely ground.

NOTE

*To make 2 tbsp ground roasted dandelion root, you'll need to start with 1½–2 cups raw roots.

Dandelion 'honey' (vegan)

Makes about 2 cups

Dandelion flowers can be and have been used to make all sorts of interesting foods throughout history: crunchy fritters, salads, infused vinegar, medicinal tea blends, even floral wine and champagne. When it comes to unusual dandelion products, though, dandelion 'honey' takes the cake.

If your lawn becomes a sea of bobbing yellow flowers during early spring, this vegan honey substitute is a fun and tasty way to obtain an unexpected yield. It's similar to maple syrup in consistency, and has a bright, lightly floral flavour which makes it perfect for drizzling over baked goods, upgrading a simple piece of toast, and sweetening tea. As always, be sure to pick dandelion flowers only from areas that are uncontaminated by chemical sprays or animals.

INGREDIENTS

4 cups dandelion petals, all bitter green parts removed

4 cups water

½ lemon, sliced

2½ cups white or raw sugar

METHOD

1   Wash the dandelion petals. Pat them dry with a tea towel (dish towel).

2   Combine the petals, water and lemon in a saucepan. Bring to the boil over high heat, then reduce the heat to medium and simmer for 30 minutes.

3   Take the saucepan off the heat and allow the liquid to steep overnight.

4   Strain the liquid through a colander lined with a scalded clean tea towel and placed over a bowl. (Compost the solids or add them to your FOGO bin.)

5   Combine the liquid and sugar in a heavy-based saucepan. Bring to the boil over high heat, stirring until the sugar is dissolved.

6   Reduce the heat to medium and simmer for about 1 hour, or until the liquid has thickened to a syrupy consistency.

7   Pour into sterilised jars and seal. The 'honey' will keep in the fridge for up to 6 months.

Magnolias

Magnolia spp. – particularly M. x soulangeana and M. stellata

There are many species and varieties of magnolias around the world, which is no surprise as they're one of the oldest flowering plants on the planet. In fact, magnolias were around before bees evolved, and it's believed that they were originally pollinated by beetles.

While all magnolia flowers are technically edible, they vary as much in their flavour as they do in their appearance. Some taste like headily spiced gingery cups of delight, while others are reminiscent of Great Aunt Janice's unrinsed, soapy cutlery. It's definitely worth tasting a sample before you harvest a basketful of blooms!

Anecdotally, *Magnolia x soulangeana* (saucer magnolia) and *M. stellata* (star magnolia) have the best flavour for general eating and preserving, so they're the focus here, but by all means, have a bit of fun playing the Russian roulette of tasting each bloom you come across!

Technically, magnolias don't have petals as we know them: instead, the fleshy parts known as tepals form the bulk of the flower, and these are the bits we're interested in as foragers.

ID POINTS

Branches and shape (1)
Magnolias are deciduous, multi-stemmed shrubs or small trees, with sprawling, gnarled branches that often grow wider than tall. The bare branches with silvery-grey bark develop pointed flower buds in late winter, followed by leaves. The fleshy, wide-spreading root system requires regular access to water and prefers deep, rich and slightly acidic soil.

Leaves
The leaves are shiny, dark green and oval-shaped with smooth edges. They grow alternately along the branches from short, stout stems.

Flowers
M. x soulangeana (2): Beautiful, lightly fragrant, blousy flowers begin as spear-shaped buds in late winter. The buds shed their outer brown papery bract, and then six to nine broad, rounded fleshy tepals emerge, typically pink or pale purple outside and white inside. These surround a central spike with firm, bristling pollen-bearing stamens below a fringed group of stigmas. The overall appearance is of a deep, rounded cup and saucer or goblet.

M. stellata (3): As for *M. x soulangeana*, but the flowers are smaller (7–10 cm/2¾–4 inches across) and feature 12 to 18 narrow tepals that emerge to form a frothy star-burst shape.

Fruits (4)
Magnolias produce compound brown to reddish-brown cone structures that burst open in summer to reveal bright orange-red seeds.

Toxic look-alikes
Very few plants could be confused with *M. x soulangeana* or *M. stellata* when viewed in their entirety. Common dogwood, English walnut and fruiting fig species look similar to Magnolias when bare in winter, but as soon as foliage emerges the similarity is lost.

Some scientists consider **magnolia seeds and seed pods** (4) to be toxic, so they are best avoided until extensive further research comes up with a definitive answer.

1

2

2 + 3

4   Considered toxic

3

Where and when to find them

Originating in East Asia, deciduous magnolia species prefer a cool to temperate climate in areas with well-draining, rich soil that's slightly acidic. They like a sunny spot, but nowhere that will get too hot or windy, and they require regular access to water.

M. x soulangeana and *M. stellata* bloom late winter to spring, with the flowers emerging before any leaves, making them a stunning addition to gardens and providing a tasty end to the 'hungry gap' of the gardener's year.

How to use them

Flavour-wise these two magnolia species sit in the 'exotic spice' range, hitting notes of ginger, clove, cardamom, citrus and even chilli. Overall, the combination is best described as 'spiced floral', which makes these species equally excellent pairings for Asian cuisine and Scandinavian-inspired baking.

Flowers: pickles, dumplings, jam, chutney, infused vinegar, gin, tea, mochi, dukkah, spice rubs, salads, baking, flavoured syrup, tempura-battered

Pickled magnolia buds

Makes 1–2 cups

Many magnolia flowers have a potent spicy, gingery, sometimes clovey flavour, so these pickled magnolia buds are a fun alternative to pickled ginger in sushi and sashimi dishes. They're equally delicious dipped in tempura batter and fried, diced and added to dumpling filling, or simply chopped and tossed through salads in place of a dressing.

Ready in two or three days, they last in the fridge for six to 12 months, so they're a great preserve to try as a method of 'catching and storing energy' while the flowers are in abundance.

INGREDIENTS

10–12 large magnolia flower buds

250ml rice wine vinegar

¼ cup white sugar

Pinch of salt

METHOD

1   Gently wash and dry the magnolia buds.

2   Remove the brown papery bracts from around the base, and any bruised tepals.

3   Cut the stems off right at the base of the buds.

4   Sterilise a large jar. Tightly fill it with buds. Using tongs or a flat knife can help you to squeeze them in.

5   Bring the vinegar, sugar and salt to the boil in a small saucepan over medium–high heat, stirring to dissolve the sugar, then reduce the heat to medium and simmer for 5 minutes.

6   Pour the vinegar solution over the magnolia buds to cover them (you may have a little liquid left over). Seal while hot and invert the jar for 1 minute to aid in sealing.

7   Allow to cool, then refrigerate.

8   Store in the fridge for 2–3 days before opening. After you've used all the buds, keep the leftover pink vinegar to use in cooking or salad dressings.

Wild plums

Prunus spp. (including *Prunus cerasifera*)

All plums come from the family Rosaceae, like apples, roses and blackberries, and fall under the genus *Prunus* along with other stone fruit such as peaches, apricots, cherries and almonds. Most cultivated species of plum are sub-species of *Prunus domestica*, believed to be the outcome of crossed *P. cerasifera* and *P. spinosa*. When left to spread by seed, plum trees will eventually revert back to their ancestors. As a result, the majority of plum trees we find in the wild yield the small, sour fruit of these two ancestral species.

Wild plum trees spend their growing energy on producing lots of slim branches and twigs each season that bear a frothing abundance of flowers and masses of small fruit that's only *just* sweet enough to tempt birds and animals to eat them and spread the seeds. Statistical probability means that even if they do a slapdash job of producing fruit, the sheer quantity is enough to continue and spread their genetic line.

I like to think of wild plum trees as first-year uni students who are interested in completing assignments with as little energy and effort as possible, so they can bunk off and head down to the pub. Wild plums' 'assignment' is to reproduce, so they'll do that, but only just. The student expression 'Ps mean degrees' means 'If you can graduate by getting just Pass grades, why bother working any harder?', and wild plums seem to have adopted this as their motto.

ID POINTS

Branches and shape

Very scrappy, congested shrubs or small trees, with many thin branches, wild plums grow to 10 m/33 feet. The bark is either mahogany or grey-brown with many small, horizontal cream or grey flecks. The tree's twiggy growth leads to an overall appearance of someone who's rolled out of bed and not bothered to brush their hair.

Leaves (1)

The leaves are oval or teardrop-shaped ('leaf-shaped'), with a large central vein and lightly serrated along the edges. The colour is mid-green or maroon changing to dark green and smooth on top, with the underside paler. They are thin and easily torn. The average length of *P. cerasifera* is 3–7 cm/1¼–2¾ inches; *P. domestica* is slightly longer.

Flowers (2)

Masses of flowers bloom along thinner stems, often in groups of three to five. The five petals, rounded and white to pink, surround one pistil and many stamens.

Fruits (3)

Oval fleshy fruits known as 'drupes' surround a hard flat seed that contains a small almond-like kernel. Each drupe has a deep indent running down one side from stem to tip, just like apricots (they're cousins, after all). The skin begins either green or maroon, and matures to yellow, orange, red, purple or blue-black, depending on the species. The fruits are often coated with a powdery white layer of wild yeast, making them excellent for fermenting with. They tend towards sourness but are perfect for fermenting, pickling and preserving.

Toxic look-alikes

All members of the *Prunus* genus are edible, so providing you check off all the ID points, you're safe to munch. Avoid cracking the plum seeds, as these contain high levels of amygdalin, which can convert to dangerous levels of toxic hydrogen cyanide if chewed and ingested.

Where and when to find them

Spread by birds and small animals, wild plums are found in gardens, in parklands and in the wild in rural areas. Once you've found one, you're likely to find others nearby. They sport flowers in spring and fruit throughout summer in most regions.

How to use them

Fruits: fresh, jam, jelly, paste, fruit leather, sauce, marinade, compote, baking, infused booze, vinegar, dried fruit, fermented pickles (umeboshi)

Wild plum barbecue sauce

Makes about 5 cups

Managing the abundance of wild plums when they're in season can be daunting because they have a high pip-to-flesh ratio, which means they're time-consuming to prepare for jam- or chutney-making. This sauce allows you to cook the fruit whole, and then use a food mill or sieve to remove the pips more quickly than if you cut them out to begin with.

This sauce is also delicious made with foraged hawthorn berries, or you can make a more Asian-inspired plum sauce by subbing out the smoked paprika and adding cardamom, star anise and orange zest instead.

INGREDIENTS

1.2 kg/2 lb 10 oz ripe plums, washed

3 cups malt or brown vinegar

3 cups water

1 tbsp crushed garlic

1 cinnamon stick

10 black peppercorns

5 whole cloves

1 bay leaf

300 g/10½ oz brown sugar

⅓ cup fish sauce

1 tsp ground smoked paprika

½ tsp salt

METHOD

1   Combine the plums, vinegar, water, garlic and whole spices in a large saucepan and bring to the boil over high heat. Reduce the heat to medium and simmer until the fruit is super-soft and squishy (20–30 minutes). Allow to cool slightly.

2   Smush the plums and liquid through a mouli or sieve* to remove the pips, skins and spices. You should end up with a pulp the consistency of runny yoghurt.

3   Transfer the pulp to a clean heavy-based saucepan and add the sugar, fish sauce, paprika and salt. Bring to the boil over high heat, stirring occasionally to dissolve the sugar, then reduce the heat to medium and simmer until the sauce has thickened (15–25 minutes).

4   Meanwhile, sterilise some bottles or jars and lids.

5   Using a funnel, pour the sauce into the hot sterilised bottles and seal immediately.

6   Cool, label, and store in a cool, dark spot. Refrigerate once opened.

NOTE

*A mouli is much easier on the biceps than a sieve, but it still takes time to remove all the skins. I start with the mouli plate that has large holes, then shift to a smaller-holed plate and pass the mixture through again.

Plum pudding brandy

Makes 6–7 cups

Wild plums tend to ripen thick and fast, so it's good to have a few ideas stashed away for preserving the glut when it happens. This simple, super-quick recipe allows you to capture seasonal flavours and turn overabundant fruit into a coveted liqueur.

Try this method with other combinations of fruit and spirit too: blackberry and elderberry gin, rhubarb gin, blood-orange rum, and raspberry vodka all work well.

INGREDIENTS

200 g/7 oz wild plums

2 bottles (700–750 ml each) brandy

½ cup sugar (white or brown)

10 cm/4 inch strip orange zest

1 cinnamon stick

2 cloves

2 green cardamom pods

METHOD

1   Wash and dry the plums.

2   Combine all the ingredients in a large glass jar.

3   Place in a cool, dark spot and shake daily for a week.

4   After a week, shake once a week for 1–2 months.

5   Strain,* pour into clean bottles and seal.

NOTE

*Save the fruit after straining your liqueur: it makes excellent fruit leather, jam, or paste to serve on a cheese platter.

Wild roses

Rosa spp.

Originating in Central Asia, over the centuries roses have become one of the world's most popular flowers, in gardens, vases and kitchens alike. There are thousands of cultivated species, all of which technically have edible parts, and it's common to find their floral fragrance in perfumes, lotions and bathroom products galore.

Being a member of the Rosaceae family (no surprises there), roses – like apples, bramble berries, quince, and even stone fruits like peach and plum that share the same heritage – feature simple pink and white five-petalled flowers and produce a fruit with multiple seeds in the middle.

When it comes to 'wild' roses, we tend to talk about two or three particular species, known for their prolific growth habit and their potential for invasive expansion. Most commonly considered invasive weeds around the world, these are *Rosa canina* (wild or dog rose), *Rosa rubiginosa* (sweet briar rose) and *Rosa rugosa* (beach rose).

All rose petals are edible, although it's often the darker coloured varieties that have the most aroma. Likewise, all rosehips (the fruits of the rose) can be eaten, but the best ripeness and flavour comes from *R. canina*, *R. rubiginosa* and *R. rugosa*. Petals can be used to make preserves, perfumes, body products, teas and more; ripe rosehips make excellent jellies, jams and desserts, and add vitamin C to hot drinks. As always, make sure plants haven't been sprayed with harmful chemicals before you ingest any parts.

ID POINTS

Leaves and stems (1)
Roses are erect or climbing deciduous shrubs, up to 5 m/16 feet 5 inches tall, featuring many long-arching smooth canes (stems) studded with backward-curving woody thorns up to 1 cm/½ inch long. The leaves are made up of five to seven ovate ('leaf-shaped') leaflets measuring 1–4 cm/½–1½ inches long, with serrated edges, glossy, hairless mid- to dark-green tops and paler undersides.

Flowers (2)
Flowers grow singly or in clusters of three to five at the end of canes or on shorter flowering spurs along canes. Flower buds feature a bulbous green base (this will become the rosehip once pollinated) topped by five fringed green sepals covering a tightly curled flower. Once opened, sepals curve down over the bulbous base, revealing five petals which are either oval or curved on the outer edge to resemble love hearts. Fully opened flowers measure 2–5 cm/¾–2 inches across, and have 10-plus yellow pistils surrounded by many stamens in the centre.

Fruits (3)
After pollination, the bulbous base of the flower swells and colours red to form smooth-skinned rosehips 1–2 cm/½–¾ inch long and oval or teardrop shaped. The sepals dry and eventually fall from the end of the rosehips. The flesh of the rosehip (which is actually a pseudo-fruit known by botanists as a hypanthium) begins firm, but after being exposed to frost and cold temperatures it undergoes 'bletting' – a process where it ripens to a paste-like consistency. When they reach this stage, rosehips are edible. Each hip houses multiple seeds surrounded by thin hairs that will cause extreme irritation of the gastrointestinal tract if ingested. Either remove all seeds and hairs before using rosehips, or leave the rosehips intact when extracting flavour and vitamins (by infusing in water, honey, alcohol etc.).

Toxic look-alikes
Always be careful when seeking to forage any red berries, hips or haws, as there are definitely some toxic ones out there. Roses are distinctive enough when in flower – a sniff is usually enough to confirm ID – but be sure to tick off all the ID points for rosehips before picking them.

Where and when to find them

Look for rose shrubs all year round among hedgerows, along rural fence lines and at the edge of forested areas. They like well-drained, rich soil with plenty of sunshine in temperate zones, but they are pretty hardy and can adapt to poor soil and limited sun.

The leaves emerge and flowers bloom from early spring to mid-summer, and the flowers lose their petals shortly after pollination. Look for ripe rosehips from late summer to late autumn.

How to use them

Flowers: tea, rosewater, soda, kefir, baking, chocolates, body products

Fruits (hips): syrup, jelly, chutney, jam, paste, Swedish dessert 'soup', tea, infused booze, oil

The irritating hairs found inside rosehips have been used by pranksters for decades to make 'itching powder'.

Dehydrated flowers

Most of the tea blends I make call for flowers of some sort (rose, calendula, cornflower, yarrow, hawthorn), so I like to dehydrate them when they're abundant for use throughout the year. As with all wild foods, I make sure to pick only flowers that I know are edible and have not been contaminated by sprays or pollution.

All rose petals are edible, but certain varieties give better flavour, so experiment to find the ones you like best. My favourites are the thorny *Rosa rugosa* and the sweet climbing rose 'Cécile Brünner'.

INGREDIENTS AND EQUIPMENT

Fresh rose petals or other petals

Flat finely woven basket (or lined baking tray)

Airtight jar

METHOD

1   Pick the roses before noon on a dry day.
2   Rinse them and pat dry.
3   Gently remove the petals. Scatter them evenly over the basket.
4   Place in a warm, sunny spot until they have dried completely (see pages 64–66). You may need to toss them occasionally to ensure they dry evenly. Large petals may take several days to dry.
5   Once dry and crisp, store in airtight jar away from heat and light.

Forager's tea

Whenever I take people out foraging, I bring along a thermos of forager's tea. Each batch is a bit different from the last, because I use whatever ingredients I've got on hand, but the basic flavour profile stays the same.

You can use fresh ingredients in place of dried ones: just be aware that ingredients shrink as they dry, so you may need to increase the amount of an ingredient if using it fresh.

If you scale this recipe up or down, keep the ratios the same. If you want to store a big batch, ensure all the ingredients are thoroughly dried before jarring up.

INGREDIENTS

2 tbsp dried rose petals

2 tbsp dried rosehips

2 tbsp dried mint leaves (any kind)

2 tbsp dried apple

1 tbsp dried orange or lemon (including the peel)

1 tbsp dried elderberry, blackberry or plum

1 tbsp dried lemon myrtle or lemongrass

½ tbsp wild fennel seeds

½ tbsp licorice root (or extra fennel)

METHOD

1   Chop or crumble all the ingredients into pieces roughly the same size.

2   For each cup of tea, use 1–2 teaspoons of the blend. Add boiling water and steep for 5 minutes or more for the best flavour. Enjoy hot or cold.

Three-cornered leek

Allium triquetrum

Three-cornered leek. Three-cornered garlic. Tricorn leek. Wild onion grass. Onion weed. Angled onion. 'That bloomin' grass that stinks the garden out'. Whatever you call it, *Allium triquetrum* is definitely a weed to view as friend rather than foe.

It belongs to the Allium family along with onions, leeks, shallots and garlic, and every part of this fragrant weed can be eaten, making it a valuable resource when understood properly. Use the greens in place of chives or spring onions; scatter the flowers as gently flavoured oniony garnishes; pickle the bulbs, flower buds and seed pods; and even shallow-fry the roots to use as crispy onion toppers on rice and noodle dishes.

Given how invasive three-cornered leek can be in creekbeds and damp green spaces, councils often spray it with weedkillers (even if they're largely ineffective), so be extra conscious of where you forage for it. Avoid areas near drain outlets and factory districts, as contaminated run-off will be sucked right up by the hungry plants.

ID POINTS

There are several excellent ID points which help you tell what's three-cornered leek and what's not, but the simplest one is its strong oniony smell. Every part of it smells, especially when broken or bruised, so if you're unsure, just crush a bit and give it a sniff.

Bulbs and roots (1)
Abundant fleshy white roots sprout from the bulbous base of the plant, like cultivated spring onion roots. The plants grow in expanding clumps of bulbs.

Leaves and stems (2)
Look for grass-green, tender strappy leaves 20–50 cm long growing in groups of eight to 12 from the bulbous base. The leaves and flower stems each have three faces and three corners (hence the common name); these are easily visible in cross-section. The leaves and flower stems bruise easily and exude a slimy clear sap when broken.

Flowers (3)
One flower stem emerges per bulb, topped by a group of eight to 10 white flowers, each with six pointed petals, suspended from delicate green stalks that emerge from papery bracts. Each petal has a green stripe down the middle, and the central reproductive parts of the flower are yellow.

Fruits (4)
Fleshy green pods have seeds that mature from white to black following pollination. The seedpods are edible, and when harvested young make an excellent alternative to cocktail onions (for tips on pickling them, see page 122).

> ### Toxic look-alikes
> Several plants can be confused with three-cornered leek, so be aware of what's growing in your region. Some, like false onion grass (*Nothoscordum borbonicum*), aren't toxic but lack flavour, whereas others, such as the common **snowdrop** (*Galanthus nivalis*) and **snowflake** (*Leucojum vernum*) (5), are toxic and should not be eaten.

5 **Toxic look-alike**

Where and when to find it

Three-cornered leek prefers cool, damp ground and will often be found near creekbeds, rivers and marshes in temperate and cool climate zones. Being perennial, the bulbs lie dormant under shallow soil during warmer months and typically send out new leaf growth from mid-autumn, with flowers emerging in mid- to late winter.

In suburban settings, look for it in boggy, dark corners of the garden or along fence lines that stay shaded during the cooler months.

How to use it

Roots: Shallow-fry, sauté with mushrooms, add to stock.

Leaves: Use chives as garnish, dry, or ferment and dry, add to pesto, pancakes and pakoras.

Flowers: Dry them, pickle them, ferment the pods, use as garnish, add to pesto or infuse in vinegar.

Fruit: Pickle, dry, add to preserves or sandwiches.

Ramped-up security

If you have ramps (*Allium tricoccum*, or wild garlic) growing near you, you can treat them largely the same way as three-cornered leek, but be aware that strict foraging laws apply to ramps in many countries. Find out what they are before harvesting this protected species.

3 + 4

Dried, fermented three-cornered leek

When I became of aware of European foragers fermenting and dehydrating ramps (wild garlic), I thought it was worth trying with three-cornered leek. The result was surprising and *so so* good: slightly salty, crunchy flakes full of umami notes. Reminiscent of wakame seaweed, it adds depth and flavour to rice dishes, soups, bread, sushi and more.

Technically you can use this method with any fermentable vegetable, but for the umami richness, alliums are best – think spring onions, chives, ramps or shallots.

INGREDIENTS

Three-cornered leek, fresh green leaf sections only

Salt

METHOD

1   Wash the leaves and shake them dry.

2   Weigh them and plonk them in a bowl.

3   Add 2–3% of the weight of the leaves in salt (see page 117 for how to calculate this).

4   Gently massage the leaves until they go a bit wilty. Leave them alone for 1 hour.

5   Massage again and leave for another hour.

6   Transfer into a clean jar. Weigh the leaves down so they are submerged in their own brine. You can use fermenting weights if you have them, but equally effective is a clean glass jar filled with water.

7   Cover the jar with a clean cloth and leave it at room temperature until the brine goes cloudy, bubbles form, and everything smells rich and flavoursome.

8   Drain the leaves (discard the brine), arrange them in a single layer on dehydrating trays or racks and dry until crisp (see pages 64–66). If you're using a dehydrator, set it to 60°C/140°F for two to four hours. If you're using an oven, set it to 100°C/200°F. Arrange the leaves on cooling racks over a tray and dry them with the oven door ajar for 1–2 hours.

9   Store the dried leaves in an airtight jar away from heat and light.

'Everything' umami spice blend

Taking inspiration from the well-known Japanese seasoning shichimi togorashi and the 'everything' bagel, I invented this spice blend one spring when the pantry was filled with ingredients I'd dried and stored over the previous months.

This rich, round blend of flavours can be used anywhere you want a spicy umami punch. Think noodle dishes, breads and crackers, eggs or avo on toast, dukkah, soup topper ...

INGREDIENTS

1–2 tbsp chilli flakes

1 tbsp ground dried blood-orange peel

½ tbsp white sesame seeds

½ tbsp nigella seeds

1 tsp poppy seeds

1 tsp ground Tasmanian pepperberry

1 tsp dried fermented three-cornered leek flakes

1 tsp ground dried porcini or shiitake mushrooms

¼ tsp ground ginger

METHOD

1   The method is so basic, it hardly deserves to be called a method. Simply mix everything together, and keep it in an airtight jar away from light and heat.

By nature, this recipe is highly adaptable, so use whatever you've got on hand to create your own special blend. Substitute similar ingredients and quantities in the recipe below to begin with, to get the right flavour balance. Here are some substitutes that work well:

Chilli flakes – cayenne, chipotle, Korean gochugaru
Ground dried blood-orange peel – dried lemon, yuzu, orange, grapefruit, mandarin
White sesame seeds – nigella, hemp, poppy or flax seeds
Nigella seeds – hemp, basil, amaranth or flax seeds
Poppy seeds – hemp, nigella, toasted sesame, basil or amaranth seeds
Tasmanian pepperberry – Sichuan, white or black peppercorns, plus lime zest powder
Dried fermented three-cornered leek – nori, wakame or bonito flakes, or dried herbs such as basil, parsley or shiso
Ginger – ground allspice, mace or nutmeg.

Chapter 5

Waste

The waste crisis that has steadily engulfed our world over the past 75 years is a massive beast, with many complicated moving parts. But there's no doubt about the fact that humans must adopt widespread, consistent improvement in the way we reduce and manage waste.

'No Such Thing
As Waste'

The behemoth that it is, 'waste' is far too broad a topic to be covered in detail in just one chapter. Many wonderful humans have written excellent books and educational resources dedicated entirely to waste that I highly recommend: Anne-Marie Bonneau, Erin Rhoads, Lindsay Miles, Dr Kate Luckins, Lauren and Oberon Carter, Alessandro Vitale, Craig Reucassel, Kathryn Kellogg … the list goes on.

What I want to do here is get you thinking about areas in your life that generate waste that you may not have considered before. Once you're aware of an issue, you're much better equipped to make gradual changes that lead to improvement.

First things first: jot down the things you would classify as 'waste' in your life. That might include things like food waste, glass, paper and metal recycling, garden waste, packaging and general waste.

Next, have a think about the areas in your household that hold resources. Anything that can be acquired, shared or wasted can be considered a resource. That might include things like water, electricity, money, time, skills and knowledge. It also includes the mega category of stuff: possessions, belongings, things.

Wherever there is a resource, there can be waste. The goal of this chapter is to get you thinking about the valuable resources you have and working towards ways you can appreciate them to the fullest of their capacity.

Once we consider something to be valuable, we're far less likely to waste it unnecessarily. This might mean that we learn to look after it better, manage its use so it doesn't get worn out, or learn to mend it if it breaks. The aim is to step away from the pernicious consumerist thinking that capitalism grooms us to hold, and reframe our thinking so we want less and value more.

Food packaging waste

'Plastic!'

When talking about waste and food, there are lots of layers to consider. Obviously there's actual food that ends up in landfill, which I'll look at on page 212, but another major generator of waste in modern kitchens is food packaging. Paradoxically, commercial food packaging plays a part in *reducing* food waste by extending the period during which food can safely be eaten. However, because of its affordability and availability, plastic has become the most common food packaging material and it is notoriously difficult to reclaim and recycle. This is especially true of soft plastic, which makes up a huge proportion of kitchen packaging waste entering landfill.

As you read in Chapter 3: Food, I use a variety of ways to reduce packaging when buying and storing food. Plastic food wrap has been around since the 1950s, with snap-lock bags following in 1964. What really grinds my gears about these is that every single bag and every piece of plastic wrap manufactured since then is *still* around, whether in its original shape or in the form of microplastics and nanoplastics that have been absorbed into the food web. And it'll still be around centuries from now, because plastic made from fossil fuel–based chemicals, which makes up the bulk of all plastic ever created, never truly decomposes.

When you end up with unavoidable plastic food packaging, take note of it. As consumers, we have the right to contact food manufacturers and suppliers with concerns over the unsustainability of their products. I've been surprised by how many stories I've heard from friends who have made complaints to bigwig food companies and found that it resulted in positive change.

When it comes to storing food well at home, I avoid plastic wrap completely, and I use snap-lock bags only if I can wash them for reuse. I repurpose as much food packaging as I can: from using meat trays to grow seedlings and repurposing resealable bags to store dehydrated food, to reusing or composting as much paper and cardboard as I can (see page 221). I favour reusable options always, and I particularly like my homemade beeswax wraps for keeping food fresh in the fridge.

Beeswax (candelilla wax is a vegan substitute) is waterproof and has antibacterial properties, making it excellent for slowing the decomposition of food. Coating fabric pieces with beeswax and using them instead of plastic wrap to wrap food locks in moisture, flavour and freshness.

Making beeswax wraps is relatively easy but can get very messy. There are several ways to make them, but this method requires only one messy melting session, and then allows you to whip up new wraps in the future using just an iron and some baking paper.

You can make the wraps with beeswax alone, but they tend not to wrap as tightly, and the wax has a tendency to flake off, meaning they require rejuvenation more frequently. Using pine rosin (processed pine-tree sap) and jojoba oil in the blend increases the suppleness and stickiness of the wraps, making them easier to use. Seek out beeswax for sale from local beekeepers online or offline. The other ingredients can often be sourced from your local whole foods or bulk-foods store.

How to make beeswax wraps

INGREDIENTS AND EQUIPMENT

Wax mixture

Medium saucepan

Metal, ceramic or glass bowl that fits on top of saucepan (as a double boiler)

85 g/3 oz beeswax pellets or candelilla wax

10 g/2 teaspoons rosin

2 tbsp jojoba oil

Baking tray

Baking paper

Glass jar, for storage

METHOD

Wax mixture

1. Combine the beeswax, rosin and jojoba oil in the bowl.
2. Half-fill the saucepan with water so it almost reaches the rim when the bowl is placed inside.
3. Bring the saucepan of water to the boil (without the bowl on top). Reduce the heat to a simmer and place the bowl on top.
4. Heat until the wax melts and the ingredients are combined. Avoid stirring.
5. Line the baking tray with baking paper, making sure it extends up the sides of the tray.
6. Carefully pour the wax mixture onto the tray and tip the tray from side to side to spread it evenly.
7. Allow to cool. Break into small pieces and store in a glass jar until needed.

Wraps

Cotton fabric

Fabric scissors

Towel

Baking paper

Iron

Aluminium foil (optional)

Wraps

1   Cut the fabric to the size you want. Useful sizes include small (20 cm/8 inches square), medium (30 cm/12 inches square), large (40 cm/16 inches square) and extra large (40 x 60 cm/16 x 24 inches).

2   Fold the towel double and place it on a work surface (e.g. a table) then place a large piece of baking paper on top.

3   Lay the pieces of fabric on top, scatter pieces of prepared wax over the top and cover with another large piece of baking paper.

4   Cover the base plate of the iron with aluminium foil to protect it from wax. Heat the iron to the cotton setting.

5   Iron the baking paper from the middle towards the edges of the fabric so the wax melts into every part of it. The fabric will look darker where it has properly absorbed the wax.

6   Remove the fabric from between the layers of baking paper and hold it in the air for a minute to dry.

How to use and care for beeswax wraps

To use your wraps, simply fold a wrap around the item you want to store, and hold the overlapping edges firmly together for a short time. The heat from your hands will soften the wax mixture, causing the fabric to stick to itself and thus sealing your package.

+   Wash wraps with a sponge or cloth wet with *cold* water and a dab of gentle dishwashing liquid. Air dry. Ensure wraps are completely dry before storing.

+   Keep away from sun and heat. This means *not* using them in a microwave or oven.

+   When a wrap loses its 'stick', rejuvenate by repeating steps 2 to 6 above.

Food waste

Most people's go-to idea for dealing with food waste is to compost it. We'll look at composting more on page 221, but if food scraps are the main resource going into your compost, it may not actually be the best solution for you. Why not try one of these instead.

Worm farming – also known as vermicomposting – relies on several species of worms to transform food scraps into beautiful black fertiliser (called castings) and a nutrient-rich liquid (correctly named leachate, but often called 'worm tea'). Kevin Espiritu's *Epic Gardening* and Costa Georgiadis' *Gardening Australia* resources on creating worm farms are great references if you want to go down this path.

Bokashi bins are another method of managing organic waste. They use an anaerobic (oxygen-free) system and specific microbes to ferment food scraps, which can then be added to compost or soil for rapid breakdown. Bokashi bins can be costly, as they require a 'curing' stage before being emptied, meaning many households require two bins for continuous use. Their major benefit is they safely compost meat, dairy and all cooked food scraps, which regular 'cold' compost doesn't.

If you don't have the space, time or inclination to manage any of these systems, don't despair! Many gardeners need more organic matter to grow their compost heaps, so you could reach out to green-thumbed neighbours, or get in touch with community gardens or allotment gardens to see if they're looking for more compost ingredients.

EFFECTIVE WASTE-SORTING SYSTEMS

While we're looking at waste-sorting ideas, let's talk about setting up a central, effective system for other types of waste too. Interestingly, the biggest hurdle for most households when it comes to managing waste effectively is uncertainty. With so much conflicting information around about what can be composted or recycled, not knowing whether something 'is allowed' in a particular bin can be seriously discouraging.

The key is to keep it simple, and make it easy to use. Design a system that doesn't ask too much of anyone in terms of effort or attention, and it's more likely to be followed. Use bins and containers that are big enough for your needs, label them with simple pictures, and put them in an area that's easy to access. If you're a bit shaky in the artistic department, there's a downloadable file of labels you can print and use on theurbannanna.com.

Obviously the categories in your system will rely on what waste management facilities you have access to and your space, but here's a list of things to consider:

+ Glass jars for reuse

+ Glass for recycling

+ Cardboard and paper for compost

+ Cardboard and paper for recycling or reusing

+ Hard plastics (e.g. containers) for recycling or reusing

+ Compost ingredients (see page 222). No meat, no fish, minimal sloppy food. Nothing that attracts rodents

+ Food for the worm farm (fresh and cooked food scraps). No dairy or meat

+ Food for the chooks (leafy veg, crushed cooked egg shells, stale bread, fruit scraps)

+ FOGO bin (as specified by council)

+ Bokashi bin

+ Light globes

+ Batteries

+ Soft plastics

+ Medicine blister packs

+ Clothing and fabrics

+ Make-up and toiletry containers.

Comparison is the thief of joy

Erin Rhoads, author of Waste Not: Make a big difference by throwing away less, *@therogueginger, Australia*

'I have found a deep joy and freedom in not "keeping up with the Joneses" and society's expectations. I've learned valuable skills, created connection within my community and forged a deep relationship with the natural world. The shifts I've made just make sense to me, and I couldn't imagine going back to how I used to be.

'I have physical disabilities but since I've been on my journey to reduce my waste for over a decade, I've learned what works for me and my family and what doesn't. The biggest barrier can be simply comparing your life to that of someone else who has more accessibility. For example, I can't do as much cooking or gardening as others, and I can't eat fermented foods. But I prioritise other areas: we look within our cupboards, fridge and fruit bowls before making a shopping list for the week, to figure out what food needs to be used up first. For us a meal plan and shopping list helps keep food waste down to virtually nothing. The only food waste is from meals the kids might not finish, egg shells, and some bones – and this all ends up in our backyard compost.'

How to make stock and stock powder

Whether it comes in non-recyclable cartons or cube form, commercially made stock creates a waste challenge. One way to get around that, and to reduce your household food waste at the same time, is to make your own stock using food scraps. Making stock this way means you get as much use as possible out of the food you buy and grow; you get 'free', tasty and tailored stock; you don't generate waste from commercial stock packaging; and your overall waste output is greatly reduced.

At its core, stock is just water that's absorbed the flavour of a mix of ingredients. Depending on what you'll use the final stock in, you can make just about any type you like: vegetable, chicken, beef, fish, corn or onion to name a few.

This no-fuss recipe allows you to collect scraps over time, and then simmer up a big pot. Freezing the final result means you'll have delicious homemade stock on hand for ages. If you're making plain veggie stock, you can even make a dried stock powder from the leftover scraps at the end!

INGREDIENTS

Vegetable scraps, peelings and stalks

Herb offcuts and stalks

Water

NOTE

*To make stock powder from the scraps left in the strainer, blitz the scraps along with a handful of herbs, half an onion and a few peeled garlic cloves, then spread them out on dehydrator trays and dry until crisp. Blitz in a food processor to form a powder and keep in an airtight jar in the pantry. Use to add an extra oomph of flavour to soups, sauces, pies, dips and more.

METHOD

1   Find a container that holds half the volume of your stockpot or largest saucepan. Pop it in the freezer and collect veggie scraps in it over a few days or weeks.

2   Once the container is full, chuck the scraps into the stockpot and fill with water.

3   Simmer over low heat for several hours.

4   Once it smells like good stock, strain* and cool.

5   Pour into ice-cube trays or jars, and freeze. If using jars, fill only ¾ full or the glass may crack as it freezes.

Work with what you've got

Anne-Marie Bonneau, author of The Zero-Waste Chef: Plant-forward recipes and tips for a sustainable kitchen and planet, *@zerowastechef, United States*

'Our front yard, which was a lawn long ago (before we let the drought kill it), is now filled with drought-tolerant native plants. We also installed a laundry-to-landscape greywater system that waters our plants (it requires specific detergent and I never send the greywater out to the yard if the load contains any synthetic fabric). We save a lot of what grows in the yard – seeds, stalks and branches to make supports for vegetables, logs for hügelkultur. We installed solar panels and have switched out two gas appliances to electric. Oh, and we hang our laundry to dry outside.

'Challenges for us often centre on other people. I can't control what my children bring into my home when they visit: they aren't as hardcore into zero-waste living as I am. Luckily they're pretty much on board with the program, though, so it's not too difficult. Living with others requires compromise.'

Garden waste

Most gardens generate a few distinct types of waste, the most common being organic, plastic and structural. Organic matter can include plant matter, manure and food waste; plastic usually comes from packaging of one sort or another; and structural is quite often the sort of stuff that accumulates and only becomes an issue when it's time to move.

Composting is the go-to method of dealing with organic garden waste. To compost effectively, you need to have a mixture of 'brown' (carbon-rich) and 'green' (nitrogen-rich) materials, otherwise you'll quickly become the owner of an impressively unpleasant pile of sludge. Have a read of the simple system on page 221 if you're keen to get your own compost going.

Plastic garden waste turns up in gardens as pots, bags, tools, packaging, labels etc., and if you're not careful, these can break down into microplastics or nanoplastics and eventually become part of your soil. Given the worrying evidence showing that microplastics can be absorbed by fresh produce (carrots and apples being among the worst affected), if you want to grow food to be healthier, better to keep plastics as far away from your garden as possible.

HOW TO REDUCE PLASTIC IN THE GARDEN

+ Avoid buying plastic-wrapped potting mix. Instead, make compost, start a worm farm to process food scraps, and collect fallen leaves. Combine these to make your own potting mix.

+ Ditto plastic-wrapped soil mix. Use no-dig growing methods instead.

+ Make your own seed-starting medium. I use Milkwood Permaculture's recipe: 2 parts sifted compost, 2 parts coir (coconut fibre), 1 part worm castings, 1 part sand and a sprinkle of aged manure.

+ Skip the plastic-wrapped seeds and seedlings. Instead, collect seeds, swap with gardening friends, and start them in seedling pots made from cardboard or paper.

+ If you're using plastic pots, make sure they're UV stable, look after them, and reuse them again and again.

+ Ditch the plastic spray bottles and big bags. Make (or collect) your own fertiliser from worms, weeds, seaweed, chooks, sheep, rabbits or guinea pigs.

+ Choose metal or wooden tools.

+ Use wood, metal and natural-fibre materials for support structures.

When it comes to structural waste, I mean lattice, climbing frames, greenhouses, pots, raised-bed edging, stakes, that kind of stuff. If they're just things you don't need any longer, rehome them with local gardening groups, permaculture communities, neighbours, schools and tip shops.

If you have plastic structural waste, it'll exist for at least another 400 years, so try to take care of it and rehome it rather than sending it to landfill to become microplastics. If you've got timber or natural-fibre structural waste, check whether it's something that could be composted, or used in a hügelkultur bed, or as mulch. Things made from metal or glass are usually quite easy to rehome, but if not, investigate what recycling options are available.

1

2

2 (optional)

3

5

There are many ways you can make compost, and while each method may look slightly different, the basic principles remain the same: mix carbon and nitrogen materials with some air and moisture, then let the microbes and fungi take over.

As a busy person who rents, composting has been one of my biggest challenges to overcome, as a lack of time and the fragile security of not knowing how long I'll be able to stay at each rental property means I'm less able to commit to larger composting systems (such as a three-bay hot compost).

The solution I've finally landed on is this compact, low-fuss system using 60 litre/16 gallon plastic bins, many of which I found secondhand. They're small enough that I can quickly bag up the contents and stack the bins if I need to move to another place, and having several on the go means I'm able to harvest completed compost more often. I can spread them around the garden if I'm short on space, and they're cheap and easy to make, so I can expand my system if I need to without it being a major drain on my finances and energy.

How to make a compost bin

INGREDIENTS

60–75 litre/16–20 gallon bin (trash can) or drum with a lid

Electric drill

Saw

Carbon and nitrogen materials for composting (see page 222)

METHOD

1   Use a 20–25 mm/¾–1 inch drill bit to drill holes all around the sides of the bin, roughly 15 cm/6 inches apart. (Leave the lid on to support the bin while handling).

2   Remove the base of the bin with the saw. If you're worried about rodents getting into your compost, secure some chicken wire over the open base

3   With the lid on, and using a twisting motion, bury the bin 4–5 cm/1½–2 inches deep where you want to use it.

4   Fill the base of the bin with a deep layer of carbon materials, then add a slightly thinner layer of nitrogen materials.

5   Continue to alternate carbon and nitrogen materials in layers (three parts carbon to two parts nitrogen) until the bin is full (this may take weeks or months). Keep the contents damp (but not wet).

6   Aerate once a fortnight by twisting a garden fork or compost twirler through the contents.

Where you place your compost bin will affect how long it takes for your compost to be ready. In a shady, cold spot, it can take up to six months to break down. In full sun (e.g. in the middle of a garden bed), it may be ready in as little as six weeks.

Carbon-rich materials

+ Straw (I prefer pea straw)
+ Lucerne hay
+ Dried leaves and small twigs
+ Shredded paper and cardboard (no glossy print, as it contains nasties that shed microplastics)
+ Finely chopped hair – pet or human
+ Dried lawn clippings (not from weedy lawns)
+ Shredded egg cartons
+ Eggshells (dried and blitzed to a powder)

Nitrogen-rich materials

+ Compost
+ Worm castings
+ Aged animal manure
+ Kitchen scraps (go easy on these)
+ Fresh lawn clippings (not from weedy lawns)
+ Fresh green leaves, shredded
+ Tea leaves (watch out for microplastics)
+ Coffee grounds

Water: too precious to waste

Continued and predicted fluctuating weather and climate patterns clearly point towards a future where water will become a much more widely valued resource. We may be a while off *Mad Max* territory, but that's no reason to squander what we have now.

Less than 0.5% of the water on Earth is useable fresh water, and around half the world's population is subject to severe water scarcity for part of every year. Fresh water isn't just used for drinking; it plays an integral role in agriculture, food production, manufacturing, energy, medicine, and waste management and is intrinsically linked with biodiversity health. Because of the inevitability of population increase, it's vital that we all start reducing the amount of water our lifestyle requires.

The simplest way to start is to reduce your use, and make the most of it. I sometimes imagine I'm camping with a limited supply of water: I find it helps me to be more mindful. Here are some things to try.

WAYS TO MINIMISE WATER USE

+ Install water-saving showerheads.

+ Reduce the water level in baths by 2 cm/¾ inch. In a small tub, that equals over 11 litres/3 gallons saved.

+ Use a timer to help you take shorter showers. Or, play a specific-length playlist so you know when to turn the water off.

+ Reconsider how often you shower. We're conditioned to believe it should be daily, but unless you sweat a lot because you're very active, the science says two or three times per week is better for your skin.

+ Set appliances to 'water saving' mode.

+ Use a front-loading rather than a top-loading washing machine.

+ Install a toilet with a half-flush button. If that's not possible, add a sealed, full 1 litre/1 quart water bottle or a regular house brick to the cistern: it'll reduce the amount of water refilled after every flush.

+ Turn the tap off when brushing teeth.

+ Hand-water gardens rather than using sprinklers (which often run longer than needed), or install drip-irrigation.

WAYS TO STACK FUNCTIONS
WITH WATER

+ Use a bucket to collect cold water as your shower water heats up. Use this to clean, mop floors, water veggies and even fill a top-loading washing machine.

+ Find a tub that fits in your kitchen sink. Capture water when waiting for the hot tap to run hot, washing produce, and even washing dishes (use greywater- and septic-safe detergents). Reuse the clean water as for shower water. If it's sudsy, use it on ornamental plants or trees.

+ Save the water you use to cook veggies. Use it in baking (match the flavours, of course), to make stock, and to water plants.

+ Use cooled bath water to water ornamental plants, trees or indoor plants (if you use greywater-safe body products).

Small steps and
simple solutions
Elizabeth Wickham, a town planner who works from home, Australia

'I strive to live sustainably by choosing eco-friendly cleaning products, opting for items with minimal plastic packaging, and composting most food waste. We have a simple system that's easy and visible in the pantry which makes sorting waste automatic for the whole family. I planted native and drought-tolerant species in the garden to reduce reliance on watering and attract native birds. We also installed a water tank to flush toilets, which saves heaps of mains-fed water with a family of four.

'I should buy more of my groceries in bulk-food and local independent stores to reduce packaging, but it is significantly less convenient, especially when we're busy. Balancing work, family and other commitments can make it hard to prioritise eco-friendly choices at times. Despite the difficulties, I make an effort to incorporate small, sustainable actions into my daily routine whenever possible.'

Know your stuff

Stuff, and humanity's consumption of stuff, is directly connected to the climate crisis. As I said in Chapter 2: Energy, energy is embodied in everything we touch and do. When it comes to stuff, there are multiple layers of embodied energy, which can be described as 'energy involved in producing a useable object'.

This includes the energy involved in obtaining raw materials, extracting and transforming them into useable materials, manufacturing, packaging, transport, storage, sales and marketing. Then there's the human power used in every stage of this. And then there's the energy involved in you earning money to afford the item, energy used managing your money (often digital these days), energy you use for transporting and storing the item ... you get the picture. There's never 'just a little' anything, yeah? There's always energy behind it.

I broadly lump my thoughts about stuff into these four categories:

1   How I think about stuff

2   How I obtain stuff

3   How I make stuff last

4   What I do with stuff at the end of its life.

How I think about stuff

+   Apply self-regulation (and accept feedback) – that's permaculture principle 4. I assess want vs need, see if I can make do with something else, and ask if I can delay acquiring new stuff.

+   Plan ahead so I have time to explore secondhand options.

+   Plan ways to disengage with problematic stuff; e.g. fast fashion, appliances and technology, pastimes (crafting is full of waste just waiting to happen).

How I obtain stuff

+   Shop at home first. This includes an occasional bit of 'making do' as well.

+   Borrow, rent, trade. Find out whether I can source it from my Community. Buy Nothing, Good Karma Network and permaculture groups online are great for this.

+   Buy secondhand first. I use op shops, estate sales, flea markets, tip shops, eBay, Etsy and local trading-post publications.

+   If buying new, I do some research into the ethical and sustainability background of the seller and the item.

+   I buy from local stores and sellers to keep my shipping carbon footprint down.

+   Buy stuff that's low on 'planned obsolescence': assess whether it's something that can be repaired if it breaks.

How I make stuff last

+   Take care of it!

+   Use as per instructions.

+   Store carefully.

+   Clean and service it.

+   Use gentle cleaning substances and materials.

+   Don't overwash clothes. It's not necessary to wash everything after one wear!

+   Have 'uniforms' for different jobs: gardening, work, exercise, relaxing, sleeping. Change between them as appropriate. This reduces unnecessary wear on clothing.

+   Fix, mend, repair. Learn different methods of fixing stuff, e.g. patching vs darning.

+   I use the repair options around me: cobblers mend shoes, craft stores can service sewing machines, Repair Cafes can fix just about anything!

Into the woods

Johnny Juhl, bushcrafter, @simple.woodsman, Denmark

'I don't buy much; I always look for options where I might be able to produce something myself. I reuse a lot of stuff, so the household doesn't need much and I produce very little waste. I'm often wearing clothes that I wore 20 years ago. It might be a bit odd for some people – but my personality doesn't depend on what I'm wearing.

'I don't like the blind consumer behaviour most people have in this world. You can't change anything – or the opinion of others – unless you are willing to make changes in your own life. It's near impossible to do this on a full scale when it's embedded in a modern world system. So it's up to all of us to make some changes and model that to encourage others.'

MENDING CLOTHES

Learning to mend clothes you already own and love is a brilliant way to reduce your dependence on fast fashion. Not only will you reduce demand for new clothes, you'll reduce the quantity of textiles entering the waste stream.

There are as many ways of mending clothes as there are types of fabric, and many books and resources freely available for when you want to try a few different methods. Of particular note are *Modern Mending* by Erin Lewis-Fitzgerald and *Visible Mending: Repair, renew, reuse the clothes you love* by Arounna Khounnoraj.

I considered trying to teach you how to darn a sock here, but it is incredibly challenging to write accurate, user-friendly instructions for hand-sewing skills, and besides, I also thought it might be more useful for you to know a bit about the range of different mending techniques out there. That way, when you have a piece of clothing that needs fixing, you can find the style that suits your needs best, and then do some targeted research for instructions on that style.

Most of the mending techniques described on these pages are what's called 'visible mending', where you're making a feature of your work rather than trying to hide it. They can be adapted to make them less visible, if you'd rather keep your mending skills on the down-low. For example, choosing a matching thread colour rather than a contrasting one will go a long way towards hiding your stitches.

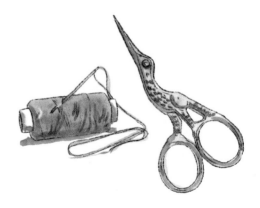

Patching

The simplest of all mends. Make it subtle, make it pop, but whatever you do, take a damaged piece of clothing and sew on a bit of fabric to make it whole again. Use fabric similar in weight and stretch to your garment's so your clothes hold their original shape. Choose to hide your stitching or make it a feature. Add patches inside the garment if you want to hide them, or stitch them on the outside for visual effect. Tuck the edges under, or overlap multiple patches for a funky textured look. Create your own patches using clothing that's damaged beyond repair: kids' socks, T-shirts and leggings with their fun printed designs are great for this. You can even make iron-on patches with special backing. Here are some ideas to start with:

+ Patch inside the garment (1)

+ Shaped patches make for fun mends (2)

+ Sew on a hand-embroidered patch (3)

+ Elegant sashiko patching is designed to reinforce worn fabric before major damage occurs (4)

+ Basic sashiko patching is great for mending the inseam and seat of jeans and work pants (5)

+ Use boro patches to both repair and reinforce – you can add and overlap more patches over time (6)

+ Do some decorative stitching (10)

Machine mending

Machine mending typically combines internal patches and machine stitching to repair tears and reinforce worn areas. It's particularly good for mending jeans and tougher fabrics.

+ Zigzag stitch (7)

+ Straight stitch (8)

Bias binding hems (9)

Technically, this is just a type of patching, but it makes use of long, thin fabric strips that are cut from fabric in a certain way to make them stretch, which is perfect for going around worn curved areas of garments such as necklines and cuffs. You can buy bias binding ready made (it's often available cheap from the op shop), or have a go at making your own.

Fixing ladders and pulls

Y'know when a jumper snags on something and a thread is pulled so it dangles annoyingly outside the garment? Or worse still, breaks and causes the fabric to unravel, leaving behind a 'ladder' that threatens to stretch from neck to navel? Well, both of those are fixable problems! It'll depend on the fabric and the size of the damage, but it's possible to mend both ladders and pulls: a quick online search will pull up all manner of videos to step you through it. Tools like latch hooks are useful for mending ladders and pulls.

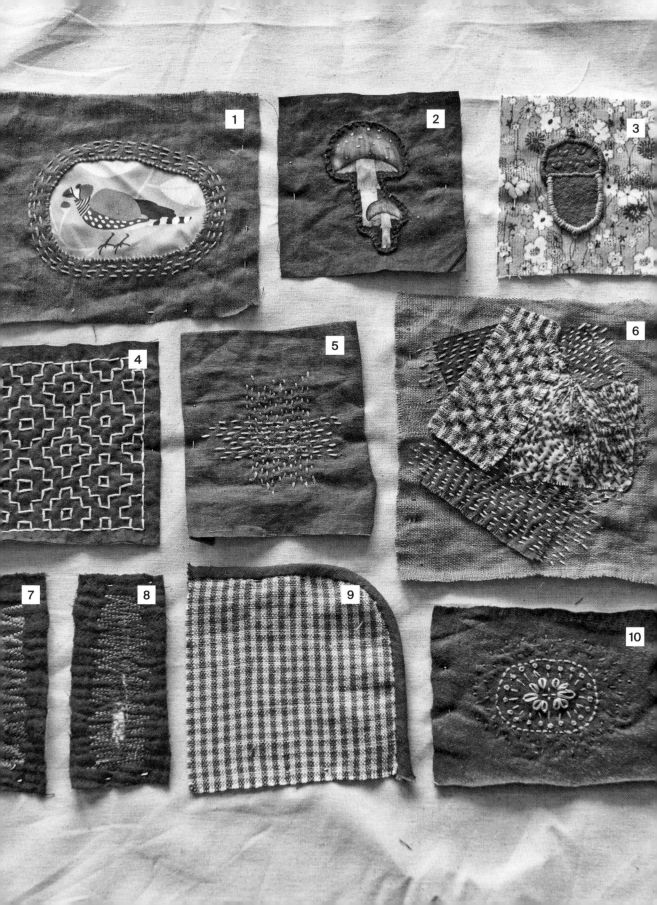

Felt mending (11)

A sort of cross between darning and patching, felt mending uses woollen fibres and a stabby tool to create a patch that is literally felted to the garment. There are special natural fibres you can buy for felting, but you can also use frayed knitting wool, or even unravel an old unwanted jumper or scarf from the op shop to obtain a yield of suitable fibres. It's best suited to small areas of mending.

Darning

Darning essentially creates a patch in situ on your garment. In this way it's different from patching, which involves making a patch separately and then sewing it on. There are lots of different darning styles, all typically done on knitted (rather than woven) fabrics. The finer the fabric, the more intricate the darning, so there's a point where it just becomes easier to patch a knitted garment than to attempt darning. Here's a mini-encyclopedia of the most common darning stitches and techniques.

+ Standard classic darning uses long, straight stitches that weave over and under each other, often over a hole (12)

+ Honeycomb darning is stitched in a spiral. It's a version of Scotch darning used to mend a rounded shape. (13)

+ Scotch darning stitch creates a weave that resembles traditional fishing nets, or chain-link fencing. Good for larger holes. (14)

+ Swiss darning allows you to fill out worn areas of fabric by mimicking the original knitted stitches. It uses threads of the original garment as a scaffold. (15)

+ Stocking-web darning is a way to use Swiss darning techniques over a torn or holey area of a garment. It involves stitching a scaffold first. (16)

WHAT I DO WITH STUFF AT THE END OF ITS LIFE

+ Give it a new home! If it's still useable, I find someone who can make use of it. Op shops, flea markets, online sharing groups ... noticing a pattern here? It's all the places you would look for something secondhand!

+ Investigate store initiatives for recycling or trading in things I no longer need. Ikea has a buy-back scheme; Nespresso (as much as I hate pod machines) has a recycling process where pods are separated and recycled and composted accordingly.

+ Find out where to recycle tricksy stuff like make-up packaging, pens, toothpaste tubes, batteries, light globes etc. It's possible!

The final word on stuff is to encourage you to think clearly about how you'll manage an item once it's reached the end of its life or use to you. We've reached the age where we *have* to take responsibility for the stuff we bring into our living systems, and that means honouring the embodied energy of it when it comes time to move it on.

Useful tools

While you don't need many specialised tools to mend clothes, a darning mushroom can make mending woollens easier. You can just as easily use a small ball or even an orange – whatever gets the job done.

Chapter 6

Moving

Around the world, people move house multiple times in their lives. In the UK, the average number of times is eight; in the US, it's 10; in Australia, it's a whopping 13 times. Given that moving is considered to be among the top five most stressful events in a person's life (up there with the death of a loved one, major illness, divorce, and job loss), that's a fair whack of time we spend being stressed.

There are so many varied factors that affect how and why someone might have to move that there's no one way to magically make it easier. That said, one factor that consistently seems to ease the burden is support. Whether it be from family, friends, employers or neighbours, support is vitally important to getting through a move, so it's well worth planning ahead and putting in scaffolding so that when it comes time to move, you feel like you've got good support around you.

The reality of moving – particularly for singles and those with health challenges or disability – is that it takes roughly six months to get from being settled at one place to being settled at the next. And the various fees, goods and services involved in that process can easily add up to several thousand dollars. It's about so much more than the moving truck hire!

The hidden costs of moving

+ Moving boxes and packing materials

+ Salary lost while taking time off to 'save money' by packing everything yourself

+ Steam cleaning of carpets and curtains

+ Flea-bombing to eradicate pests (if you have pets)

+ Cleaning services

+ Cleaning equipment and supplies

+ Maintenance and damage repair

+ Rubbish removal

+ Connection and set-up fees for water, gas, electricity, internet and phone services

+ Physical therapy for injuries and strains sustained while packing and moving

+ Bond

+ Fuel for going to and from the old and new place

+ Buying prepared meals and takeaway while you're busy and kitchen things are packed away

+ Materials to set up new gardens or play spaces for children or pets.

If we start considering factors like mental health, physical resilience and the environmental impact of moving, the costs can rack up even further. So let's look at some ways to make moving a less stressful and less costly endeavour.

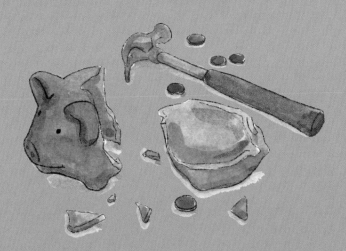

House hunting

It's impossible to reduce the intricacies of house hunting to one set of examples, as every situation is unique. You might be looking for a single bedroom in a sharehouse, seeking a tiny house on wheels, moving in with a partner, buying a house, or renting a granny flat in an intentional community – global housing is as diverse and individual as humans are.

When it comes to finding and choosing a new place to live, then, I find it most helpful to think in terms of personal values and futureproofing. This way it doesn't matter if I'm downsizing, upsizing or shifting astral dimensions – what I'll be looking for remains the same.

First, reflect on your needs. How long do you envisage living at this new place? Can you imagine it satisfying your needs for that time period? Does it have an appropriate number of bedrooms, bathrooms, enough living space, room to live, work and play? Does it have enough physical space to house the stuff that's important to you? (I always consider whether a place has enough space for the jars and baskets I own. I have a lot of them.)

Check out the fixtures and appliances – are they energy efficient? Gas vs solar hot water, electric vs gas heating, air-con vs ceiling fans. Is the place equipped to use renewable energy sources? Is there carpet in the living spaces? Do the windows have pelmets above the curtains? What features are there that mean you can rely less on powered temperature control?

Next look at the aspect. Does the place get much direct sunlight? This is important for gardening and sipping lattes in the sun, but more than that, having access to sunlit spaces means you can dry washing, preserve food by dehydrating and keep warm using passive solar energy. If you choose a place with only south-facing windows that don't get much sun (in the northern hemisphere, that means only north-facing windows), no matter how many curtains and door-seals you install, the place is going to be cold in winter, which will increase the likelihood that you'll use energy-hungry appliances and heating. A place with some north-facing spaces (south-facing in the northern hemisphere), on the other hand, affords you access to passive solar energy to use in many ways.

Note down how many shelves there are in cupboards; check whether the light globes are the energy-efficient LED type; check whether doors and windows have good draught seals; and assess what the curtains are like. This allows you to prepare for small, simple energy-saving alterations you can make as soon as you move in (Chapter 2: Energy, has lots of info on these).

Investigate how close the place is to public transport, independent food shops, community services, green spaces, work and study facilities that you use. Would you be able to ride a bike instead of drive a car? Will it cost you more money (and carbon emissions) in fuel to live there than in another place?

Lots of questions! Ultimately, though, for me it boils down to this one: Will this place make it easier or harder for me to make environmentally conscious decisions in the future? Whenever I'm lucky enough to have a choice between several rentals, I'm always going to choose the one that presents the fewest barriers to implementing small and slow sustainable actions while I live there.

Stuff and nonsense

The first step when you're looking at your stuff and assessing what to take with you when you move is to reflect honestly on whether a thing is truly valuable and useful to you. If it is, go ahead and pack it up. But if not, rather than binning it, consider some of these options for moving it on:

+ Hold a garage sale. It could be a traditional one where you price and sell items, or you could set up a free or fundraiser table where people take what they like and donate funds to a cause.

+ Give items to people you know will appreciate them.

+ Donate to op shops, schools or church communities for use in fundraising.

+ Drop off at your local tip shop.

+ List items on local online sharing forums, either for sale or to give away.

When it comes to packing, start by putting aside everything you'd need if you were going on a two-week camping trip. Check your calendar to see what activities you've got happening in the fortnight before you move, then set aside the clothes you'll need for that period. Plan to use up as many food items as you can in the weeks before the move, and set aside the equipment you'll need to cook them, along with a basic set of utensils, plates and so on. Then you'll know that everything else is to be packed!

Try to avoid buying single-use packaging materials. Online community groups are full of people giving away moving boxes after they're moved house, and they're usually in great shape after just one use. Rather than using butcher's paper or bubble wrap, 'stack your functions' (see page 12) and use every soft item you own as protective packaging.

Some of my go-to combos are:

+ **Lamps, vases and picture frames – cushions, pillows and blankets**

+ **Crockery – sheets and pillowcases**

+ **Cookware – blankets and towels**

+ **Glassware and trinkets – clothes**

+ **Bathroom cabinet contents – towels.**

Lastly, I pack anything extra valuable or precious into a small suitcase and ask a friend to look after it for a few weeks, so I'm not worried about it during the bustle of moving day.

Gardening on the go

You can never start too early when it comes to preparing a garden for a move. It's one of the first things I consider when I find out it's time to move.

It'd be ideal to be able to practise good earth stewardship and leave behind plenty of the biodiverse garden system you've created, but if the property is going to be demolished or developed, or if you have a landlord who wants a clean slate for the next tenants, it makes more sense to take your favourite plants with you.

As a renter I grow most things in pots specifically so I *can* take them with me. Deciding what to keep is largely determined by the space in the next rental. I assess and gift or donate plants I no longer want to schools and community gardens, and then work on getting the others into peak health before moving day.

As soon as you decide to move, transfer any inground plants you want to keep into large pots. Harvest any produce or flowers to enable the plants to conserve their energy for growing. Feed, prune, water and mulch potted plants. Avoid planting anything new. Consider asking friends to babysit extra special or fragile plants. Tidy the corners of the garden and sweep out soil and leaves; use these to mulch pots. Either chop and drop weeds as mulch, or use boiling water to kill them off. Get friends and Community involved. Host a working bee to tidy sheds, mow lawns, weed garden beds, and sweep and clean around the outside of the property.

On moving day, I hire a trailer or ask a friend with a ute or truck to help move potted plants. Be aware that plants need protection when travelling, so if they're going to be exposed to high speed and wind, cover them with sheets, tablecloths and blankets. Use string to reduce their bulk by tying branches close to the trunk or stem. And I always transport fragile plants inside a vehicle to reduce the stress on them.

Priority moving
Tanya, single, rents a small home solo on acreage, Australia

'Put your personal sustainability first. *Ask. For. Help.* Pack a priority box. This box is for things that will make you feel at home and at ease in your new place. My box always includes the kettle and my preferred tea. A couple of cups and mugs. A plant. A crystal to hang in the window for rainbows. Some incense or a candle with a smell I like. A speaker so I can play my music. And a favourite jumper or blanket.

'If you're friends with your neighbours, you can pass on what you can't take – in my most recent case, plants, soil and garden beds.

'Ultimately? Have less stuff. Be good at tetris.'

Understanding the pH of cleaning solutions

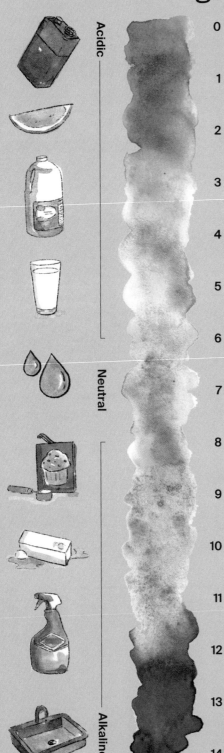

Acidic

Neutral

Alkaline

0 **Battery acid** Can be used to clean concrete, but white vinegar does the same with far less environmental impact.

1 **Citric acid or lemon juice** Wash glass, mirrors, enamel sinks and toilets. Disinfect. Deodorise dishwasher.

2 **White vinegar** Wash windows, polish silver, unclog drains, kill mould, mildew and weeds.

3

4

5

6 **Milk** Clean leather, remove ink stains on fabric.

7 **Pure (deionised) water** Clean windows, floors, solar panels, exteriors without any other chemicals.

8

9 **Baking soda** Clean stovetop, oven, grill, tiles and grout. Gently scrub metal. Clean sinks and drains, remove oils and fats.

10 **Detergent or castille soap** Wash dishes, clean kitchen counters, use as shampoo and body soap.

11

12

13 **Bleach** This is not a cleaner but a disinfectant.

14 **Drain cleaner** Can be used to clean drains, but baking soda and boiling water works just as well with less environmental impact.

Cleaning

After all the boxes have gone, it's usually time to clean. There are benefits to employing professional cleaners – it's less work for you, the job will be completed quickly, and if they're a rental-specific cleaner, they'll often come with a guarantee that your agent will be happy with the job. But there are downsides too: cleaners can be costly, they're less likely to service just one or two rooms in a sharehouse, you have little control over which products they use, and they often opt for pretty non-eco choices.

As a general rule, cleaning solutions rely on either acidic or alkaline ingredients to remove the wide variety of substances that we consider 'dirt'. Acids erode mineral deposits, salts and starches, while alkaline substances break down organic matter like oils, fats and proteins.

Knowing this is helpful, because it allows you to choose simple ingredients to clean just about everything. The diagram on page 244 shows the pH (acidity levels) of common cleaning substances, and provides info on how to use them for cleaning. Once you feel comfortable using some of these, you can completely bypass *that* aisle of the supermarket, the one filled with synthetic fragrances and all that plastic packaging that will remain part of the ecosystem forever after it's been discarded.

Buy washing soda or bicarbonate soda as your alkaline substance for shifting greasy organic matter, and white vinegar and citric acid as your acids to disinfect surfaces and remove lime scale. White vinegar from the food aisle of the supermarket is usually 4–5% acidity, but it's also possible to buy 8% 'cleaning vinegar', which is strong enough to kill off almost all bacteria around the home. All of these products are generally available with minimal packaging from bulk-food stores these days.

If you are going to buy cleaning products off the shelf, look for those that are greywater- and septic-safe, as these they cause far less damage to waterways than others. Also look for those that are packaged in glass, metal or cardboard over plastic, and if they *are* in plastic, make sure it is refillable, reusable, or recyclable in your local waste management systems.

This cleaning solution is made with white vinegar and any lemon frames (squeezed halves or pieces) you have leftover from cooking or preserving: you can also add orange, lime or grapefruit peel if you like. The limonene in the citrus peel acts as a solvent to break down oils, and the vinegar kills bacteria as it carries away the grime. It works wonders in the kitchen and dining areas, and the zingy, citrusy smell makes the space smell lovely and fresh too.

Citrus cleaning vinegar

INGREDIENTS

Lemon frames or peels

White vinegar

METHOD

1　Add the lemon to a large jar.

2　Cover with white vinegar.*

3　Seal and leave in a cool, dark spot for a month or so. Shake the jar daily for the first week, and then once a week after that.

4　Strain the mixture through a clean tea towel (dish towel) into a clean bowl or jar.

5　Pour into a spray bottle (one with a filter at the end of the spray tube is handy to stop any rogue bits of lemon from clogging it up) and keep in the cupboard.

6　Use as a spray 'n' wipe surface cleaner.

Add a sprig of fresh rosemary or thyme, or a few cloves if you like, for added antibacterial properties.

NOTE

*If you don't have enough lemon bits to fill the jar, just use what you have. You can add more to the jar as you have them, along with extra vinegar to cover, as the jar sits for the next month.

Less is more

When you're using homemade cleaning products, avoid mixing acids and alkalis (e.g. vinegar and bicarbonate of soda). They react together chemically to produce lots of gas bubbles and ... water. You'll get better results picking one or the other.

Setting up

Once I've survived moving day, the last thing I want to do is ... Welllll, basically *any*thing other than sleep for a week. I certainly don't have energy for any side-quests when I'm still unpacking three weeks later. But there are a few things I do to set myself up for success as part of the moving process.

If you need to sign up with gas, electricity, internet and water providers for the new place, investigate the options almost as soon as it's certain where you'll be moving. Compare providers, and suss out the difference between their available plans to find out which is the most eco-conscious option. Many electricity companies now have solar, wind or hydroelectric plans, or, at the very least, an option to carbon-offset their non-renewable energy sources. Navigating all this can seem overwhelming, but if you contact a few providers and tell them you're shopping around, more often than not they'll fall over themselves to provide information. Sometimes they even throw in special deals or savings.

Lining kitchen, bathroom and laundry shelves with sturdy paper (wallpaper offcuts from op shops are ideal) protects the shelves, and means that when it's time to move again, clean-up just involves removing the paper and giving the shelves a quick wipe with hot water.

Before you start unpacking, get your waste-sorting systems up and running. Having clearly labelled collection points for things like recycling, composting and miscellaneous (light globes, batteries etc.), means you can sort as you unpack. This reduces the temptation to chuck things in landfill because you're exhausted. If you're planning on setting up garden beds or a compost system at the new place, plain packaging materials like uncoated cardboard boxes, butcher's paper and corn-based packing peanuts can go straight on those sorting piles.

When it's all over and you're finally sitting down with a cup of tea, take a moment to reflect on the move: is there anything that would have made it easier? Did you find anything more challenging than you expected? Did you end up rushing certain things and choosing less eco-conscious options or actions? Basically, think about what could have made the whole experience a bit less stressful, and more aligned with your preferred sustainability practices, and then see if there's anything you can put in place now to make the *next* move, whenever that is, better.

'Look Around'

Learning new digs

Once you're in the new place, begin learning its personality. Keep track of bills so you can work out whether something's not functioning as efficiently as it should. Notice any drafts and hot spots so you can prepare to manage them in extreme seasonal weather. Map the path of the sun across your indoor and outdoor spaces so you can maximise your use of passive solar for drying clothes, dehydrating food, and growing plants.

As soon as you and your new home are better acquainted, start working on building Community again (see Chapter 1: Community). Here's a list of things I like to do whenever I move somewhere new:

+   Go on a Community walk. Notice what resources are in my new 'hood. Earmark local independent shops, say hello to people walking their dogs, find out where the closest public transport is, identify the buildings where community groups gather.

+   Find out where the local collection points are for recyclables. Is there a cash-for-cans hub nearby? What about the local tip, or collection bins at council buildings? Do local shops have battery, light globe or e-waste recycling points?

+   Join local online groups. Permaculture, zero waste, Buy Nothing, Good Karma – all good terms to search for when you're looking to build Community that will support you in living more sustainably.

+   Find out whether local shops allow you to BYO containers when buying things like butcher and deli items, dry goods like rice, cereals, snacks and sweets, and cleaning products.

+   Join local groups that interest you – art, sport, nature etc.

+   Find out about council initiatives – maybe the council hosts tree-planting days, or runs textile collection drives, or offers subsidies on compost bins or worm farms for residents.

+   Pass on any packing materials you have no use for – keep that wheel turning!

To new beginnings

As you've probably gathered from reading *Everyday Permaculture*, there is no one way to 'do sustainability right', when so many factors affect our daily lives and circumstances. What I hope is that you now feel less daunted and more empowered to make small choices every day that contribute to a more sustainable life. Here's a reminder of how you can do that:

Community. Connect with new people, find your tribe, and value the importance of personal resources like time, knowledge and kindness.

Energy. Energy is embodied in everything we touch and see. Learn to see it, value it, catch and store it, and share it with others.

Food. We deal with food every day, so it's a great place to start making changes in your habits and actions. Make considered choices, value what you have, have a go at making things from scratch, and share your excess with your Community.

Foraging. So much food grows without our interference. We can build a stronger connection with Country and reduce our impact on nature by learning to safely become part of the broader food web.

Waste. There's really no such thing as waste, only resources that haven't found their purpose yet. Learn to stack functions and your waste problems will drastically reduce.

Moving. Change is part of life, but moving can be hard. Use it to strengthen your bonds with – and your appreciation of – Community: it'll make it so much easier to manage.

Whether you've learned to identify chickweed and make weedy green pesto, begun to transform sad wibbly veg into nutritious delicious stock, or started getting together with others to share your skills, I hope this book has got you thinking about attainably sustainable ways to live a little differently for the sake of the planet, other humans, and the future we're all a part of.

Xo
Anna

'Many Many'

'Trees Eat Us All'

Further resources

I'd love to include everyone who's inspired me, but space is very limited, so here are just some of my favourite resources for attainable permaculture living.

ALL-ROUND EXCELLENT PERMACULTURE PEEPS

Brenna Quinlan

brennaquinlan.com.au

The permaculture art activist you didn't know you needed in your life. Children's book illustrator, the artist behind *Everyday Permaculture*'s gorgeous paintings, and creator of topical, relatable drawings that spark conversation.

Formidable Vegetable

formidablevegetable.com

The eco-funk band featured throughout *Everyday Permaculture*, helping folks of all ages understand and learn about permaculture through song.

Holmgren Design, Melliodora

holmgren.com.au

Home to permaculture co-originator David Holmgren and sustainable skills expert Su Dennett. A hub of the modern permaculture movement, with oodles of educational resources.

Milkwood

milkwood.net

Internationally acclaimed permaculture educators Nick Ritar and Kirsten Bradley show regular people ways to live permaculture lifestyles in modern settings. Full of wisdom, loads of experience, really relatable teaching style.

Permaculture Principles

permacultureprinciples.com

One-stop shop for worldwide permaculture and permaculture-aligned resources.

GARDENING

Charles Dowding

charlesdowding.co.uk

Renowned no-dig gardening expert, sharing excellent knowledge about composting and growing food from seed.

Costa Georgiadis

costasworld.com.au

Australia's favourite garden gnome: TV show host, public figure, event host, and massive advocate of reducing waste, growing food and living more sustainably.

Kate Flood

@compostable.kate

Demystifying compost and providing everything you need to know to transform waste into black gold.

FORAGING AND FOOD

Adam Grubb

eatthatweed.com

Co-author of The Weed Forager's Handbook, the first Australian guidebook I owned; it sparked my confidence to learn more. A permaculture educator invested in helping others access food more sustainably.

Diego Bonetto

diegobonetto.com

Combining European and Australian knowledge about wild edible foods, and teaching others through books, events and online content.

Pascal Baudar

urbanoutdoorskills.com

Author of the Wildcrafted book series and an expert in foraging, fermenting, pickling, brewing, wild clay pottery and ancient wild grain.

Sandor Katz

wildfermentation.org

'The godfather of modern fermentation', astoundingly knowledgeable, has the answer to any and every question about fermenting you could dream up.

WASTE AND REPAIRS

Anne-Marie Bonneau

zerowastechef.com

One of the world's best-known zero-waste activists. Author, blogger, super-relatable sharer of everyday low-waste living.

Erin Fitzgerald

modernmending.com

Modern mender extraordinaire, author and teacher, sharing ways to reduce fashion waste by using different mending techniques.

Lyndsay Miles

treadingmyownpath.com.au

Australia's first zero-waste blogger turned public educator and author, transforming lived experience into inspiring guidance.

Acknowledgements

Writing a book has been an awesome experience, and I've learnt so much throughout the process. I'm so grateful to everyone who came on the journey with me: I'd have been a soggy, wibbly mess by now without you all.

The Hardie Grant Explore team has been wonderful to work with: kind, caring, good at only slightly glazing over when I went into full autie-explainey mode, and generally taking such good care of this book. Thank you Melissa Kayser for approaching me with the chance to work on this project, and thank you Danielle Dominguez for overseeing it with your Scandi-trained eye. Amanda Louey, thanks for running the show on a topic so broad and new to you and for enjoying sharing photos of your cat as much as I do: neither is easy, and you achieved them both with aplomb. Celia Mance, your design created such a beautiful home for all my ideas to live in, and I love it.

To Kerryn Burgess, you've been the editor of my dreams, and I can't get over how nourishing it's been to have someone know my thoughts so well, and to tame my words so lovingly. Thank you!

To my beautiful creative magicians, Brenna Quinlan, Kirsten Jenkins and Rochelle Eagle: how can I even begin to express how wonderful you are?! You saw what I saw in my mind's eye and lovingly ushered it onto the pages, and it makes me so happy. I feel so lucky we got to create this visual feast together.

To the wonderful Sally and Jason: thank you so much for opening your home to the whole crew for a day of photography. The way you live the permaculture principles is inspiring, and that authenticity shines through in the images.

To Deb, Neil, Barb and Brad: thank you for providing me with such peaceful, comfortable spaces in which to work on different stages of the book. You can guess where I'll be bringing copies to read by the fire!

Thank you to everyone who completed surveys and contributed your thoughts and personal permaculture practices to share. I wasn't able to include anywhere near as much of these as I'd hoped, but the depth and diversity of your responses played a huge part in shaping this book.

There aren't words enough in my vocabulary to do justice to all the thanks and gratitude I want to cascade upon all my wonderful, supportive and caring friends. Arb, Baba, Dom, FPs, Jane and KPs, thank you forever and always for all the times you've listened, encouraged, comforted, workshopped and loved me in ways that made me stronger. Your friendships enabled me to achieve this enormous thing, and I love you all.

And finally, to Calle, P'Dads, Lil'Bit and my dearest strong Mamma: I'm so lucky you're my family, and I'm eternally grateful for everything you've done to help me become who I am today. Puss och stor kram. xo

Index

A

apples 129, 150–3
    Boozy blackberry and apple jam 160
    Festive spiced apple jelly 154

B

bathrooms, energy wastage 56
bedrooms, energy wastage 54
beeswax wraps 101, 209–11
bias binding hems 230
blackberries 156–9
    Boozy blackberry and apple jam 160
bottling 113
bread and butter pudding 60
bread reuse 59–63
breadcrumbs 59

C

cakes, Quick jam cake 98
catching and storing energy 33
Catie pie (weedy greens pie) 165
cat's ear 171
celery 119
ceramic crocks 102
chai latte, Dandelion-spiced chai latte 172
Cheat's dill pickles 122
chickweed 162–3
choko 75
chutney-ing 109
Citrus cleaning vinegar 256
cleaning products 245
    Citrus cleaning vinegar 246
    pH (acidity and alkalinity) 244, 245
cloth wraps 102
Community 15, 19, 250
    big 'C' and little 'c' 25
    building 39, 249
    challenges to building 32
    concept of 22
    growing your own 30–1
    how to build 28–9, 33
    importance of 26
    where to find 20
Community sharing stand 35–6
compost bin 220–1
composting 90, 217
    carbon-rich materials 222
    nitrogen-rich materials 222
contaminants 144
cordials 126

D

dandelion 168–71
    Dandelion 'honey' (vegan) 175
    Dandelion-spiced chai latte 172
darning 233
dashboard method of dehydration 66
Dehydrated rose flowers 193
dehydrating 106
    indoors 66
dill pickles 122
Dried, fermented three-cornered leek 201
drying food 64–6
dumpster diving 74

E

elderflower/elderberry 142, 143
energy 42, 250
    at home 50–6
    catching and storing 33
    personal 45–7
    sources of 44
    what is it? 44
energy wastage, reducing 50, 51–6
ethical foraging 40, 136, 139
ethical permaculture 10
'Everything' umami spice blend 202

F

false onion grass 196
felt mending 233
fermenting 113
    calculating 3% salt 117
    Cheat's dill pickles 122
    lacto-fermenting 114
    Scrap-chi (scraptastic kimchi) 118
    Summer salsa 121
Festive spiced apple jelly 154
food 70, 250
    adaptable thinking about 75
    foraging 93, 133–202
    growing 79–90
    making it last 101–13
    making your own 97–8
    meal planning 74
    peels 126
    preservation methods 105–13
    reducing waste 125
    scraptastic 128–31
    sourcing 90, 93–4, 97, 101, 102
food choices, money talks 73
food packaging waste 208
food waste 125, 131, 212
    Stock and stock powder 214

Forager's tea 194
foraging 93, 133–201, 250
    the big picture 137
    equipment 144
    ethics 136, 139
    fruit cautions 137
    laws and limits 137
    places to look 146
    plant knowledge/plant identification
        142–3, 144
    'rule of quarters' 139
    rules and etiquette 139
    safety and risks 134, 140–4
    what to look for when 146–7
    what to make with your finds 149
    wild edibles 150–201
freezer 101
freezing (preservation) 106
fridge 101
fruit foraging
    caution 137
    see also apples; blackberries;
        wild plums
fruit leather 126
fruit peels 126

G

garden waste 217–18
garlic herb croutons 63
gifting economy 39
glass jars 101, 102
growing food 79–90
    compost and worms 90, 217, 222
    getting started 79
    natural pest control 86–7
    no-dig gardening 81
    pot growing 82–5
    watering 90
    where to grow 89

H

hawkbit 171
hawthorn 143
heater or fireplace dehydration 66
home energy audit 50–6
home foraging 93
honey, Dandelion honey (vegan) 175
hot-water-bath canning 113
'hotbox' cooking 54
house hunting 239
human energy 33, 45, 47, 48

I

ice-cube trays 101

J
jamming 109
jams, Boozy blackberry and apple jam 160
jellying 109

K
kitchen, energy wastage 53–4

L
lacto-fermenting 114–17
ladders and pulls (garments) 230
lagom 19
large-scale solar dehydrators 65
laundry, energy wastage 56
living spaces, energy wastage 51–3
living sustainably 7
living systems 12

M
machine mending 230
magnolias 176–9
    Pickled magnolia buds 180
    seeds and seed pods 176
making your own food 97–8
meal planning 74
meat vs plant diet debate 73
mending clothes 229–33
moving house 235–49, 250
    cleaning the house 245
    hidden costs of moving 238
    learning new digs 249
    planning, packing and disposing 241
    preparing a garden for a move 242
    setting up the new premises 248
    see also house hunting

N
natural pest control 86–7
no-dig gardening 81
no-dig pots 84–5

O
old-school booze 63
oven dehydration 66
Oxalis 143

P
pantry 102
panzanella salad 60
parmesan crackers 62
patching 230
peels 126
permaculture
    ethics and principles 10–11
    what is it? 10

personal energy 45–7
pest control 86–7
pesto, Weedy greens pesto 166
pests and disease, spreading 137
petty spurge 162, 163
pH of cleaning solutions 244
physical safety when foraging 143
Pickled magnolia buds 180
pickles, Cheat's dill pickles 122
pickling 110
pies, Catie pie (weedy greens pie) 165
plant identification 142, 144
plant knowledge 142–3
plastic containers 101
plastic garden waste 217–18
plates 101
Plum pudding brandy 186
plums, wild 182–3, 185, 186
poison hemlock 142
pot growing 82–4
preservation methods 105–13

Q
Quick jam cake 98
quickling (quick pickling) 110

R
ramps 199
relishing 109
roses, wild 188–91
rules and etiquette of foraging 139

S
safety and risks while foraging 134, 140–4
sauces, Wild plum barbecue sauce 185
scarlet pimpernel 162, 163
Scrap-chi (scraptastic kimchi) 118
scraptastic food 128–31
seasonal foraging guide 147
seasoning blends 126
share and share alike 39
sharing stands 35–6
sign making 36
small-scale solar dehydrators 64
snowdrop 196, 197
snowflake 196
solar dehydration indoors 66
solar dehydrators 64–6
sourcing food 90, 93–4, 97, 101, 102
sow thistle 171
spice blends 126
    'Everything' umami spice blend 202
Spoon Theory 45–6
spring onions 128

stacking firewood 48
stacking functions 12, 48, 66, 75, 224
stale bread, reusing 59–63
sticky labels 102
stock 126, 214
stock powder 214
stuff 33, 226–7
    moving house 241
    obtaining it and making it last 26
    what to do with it at the end of
        its life 233
Summer salsa 121
sustainability 10
syrups 126

T
tepache 126
thinking about food 74–5
three-cornered leek 196–9
    Dried, fermented three-cornered
        leek 201

U
used plastic bags 101

V
vases 102
veggie peels 126
vinegar 126

W
waste 206–9, 250
    see also food waste; garden waste
waste-sorting systems 212–13
watering/water use 90, 223–5
Weedy green pie 165
Weedy greens pesto 166
wild carrot 142
wild garlic 199
wild lettuce 7
wild plums 182–3
    Plum pudding brandy 186
    Wild plum barbecue sauce 185
wild roses 188–91
    Dehydrated flowers 193
    Forager's tea 194
worms 90

Y
yoghurt making 76–8, 97

Published in 2025 by Hardie Grant Explore, an imprint of Hardie Grant Publishing

Hardie Grant Explore (Melbourne)
Wurundjeri Country
Level 11, 36 Wellington Street
Collingwood, VIC 3066

Hardie Grant Explore (Sydney)
Gadigal Country
Level 7, 45 Jones Street
Ultimo, NSW 2007

hardiegrant.com/explore

A catalogue record for this book is available from the National Library of Australia

Hardie Grant acknowledges the Traditional Owners of the Country on which we work, the Wurundjeri People of the Kulin Nation and the Gadigal People of the Eora Nation, and recognises their continuing connection to the land, waters and culture. We pay our respects to their Elders past and present.

For all relevant publications, Hardie Grant Explore commissions a First Nations consultant to review relevant content and provide feedback to ensure suitable language and information is included in the final book. Hardie Grant Explore also includes traditional place names and acknowledges Traditional Owners, where possible, in both the text and mapping for their publications.

Everyday Permaculture
ISBN 9781741179033

10 9 8 7 6 5 4 3 2 1

Project editor
Amanda Louey

Editor
Kerryn Burgess

Proofreader
Eliza Webb

Design and Typesetting
Celia Mance

Photographer
Rochelle Eagle

Stylist
Kirsten Jenkins

Illustrator
Brenna Quinlan

Production manager
Simone Wall

Colour reproduction by Kerry Cooke and Splitting Image Colour Studio

Printed and bound in China by LEO Paper Products LTD.

The paper this book is printed on is certified against the Forest Stewardship Council® Standards and other sources. FSC® promotes environmentally responsible, socially beneficial and economically viable management of the world's forests.

All images are copyright Anna Matilda except for the following.
p. 87 (Lacewing): Shutterstock/Henri Koskinen, (Mites): Shutterstock/Catherine Eckert; p. 163 (5): Shutterstock/Martin Fowler; p. 177 (4): Shutterstock/Iva Vagnerova; p. 227: Shutterstock/Lia_t.